For
Susannah

A Short History of Secularism

'It is widely recognised that organised religion has much less political power and imaginative weight in Britain today than it held a century or so ago and that in that sense we live in a much more secular society. Few of us have much idea how to reconcile that recognition with the fact that most Britons still stalwartly identify themselves as believing Christians, even if they seldom or never go to church. Graeme Smith's thoughtful book is a bold and intriguing attempt to explain why each is true and interpret how we have reached this outcome and what it means for the continuing presence of Christianity in the lives of even the robustly incredulous.'
John Dunn, Professor of Political Theory, University of Cambridge

'Graeme Smith presents a fresh perspective on an increasingly topical question: what is secularism? Smith argues that secular thought is heavily dependent on Christian assumptions – so much so that liberal morality, for example, is hard to understand except as a Christian inheritance. Even those who reject his strong claim that modern western ethics is bound to be Christian – as I do myself – can learn much from the alternative view of secularisation which Smith develops.'
John Gray, Professor of European Thought, London School of Economics

'In *A Short History of Secularism*, Graeme Smith has given us a lucid and strikingly original account of secularisation. The book confounds both secularisation theorists who announce the disappearance of Christianity and Christians who claim a religious identity untouched by historical change. By contrast, Dr Smith's own interpretation makes sense of the broad sweep of Western history and the shared moral convictions of modern liberal democracies. It offers a departure from the cautious revisions of Weber and Durkheim that have dominated the literature. This bold and provocative book deserves to be widely read; and, if widely read, it will certainly be widely discussed.'
Robin W. Lovin, Cary Maguire University Professor of Ethics, Southern Methodist University

'Graeme Smith's book offers fascinating insights into Western secularism. His engagement with key theorists and theories gives the reader a clear and accessible map of secularism as this has been understood in Western thinking. On his map he helpfully charts the chief patterns of religious engagement and disengagement within Western society. There are important chapters here on Christian identity, popular religion in the medieval period, Victorian Christianity and contemporary religious belief. Smith writes well and lucidly about current debates in sociology of religion regarding the secularization thesis. He also discusses topics that are of great interest to modern political theorists. *A Short History of Secularism* will be mandatory reading for both undergraduate and postgraduate students in religion and politics who seek an understanding of the concept and theories of secularism in the West.'
Angie Pears, Senior Lecturer in Religion, Theology and Culture, Oxford Brookes University

'Graeme Smith's book is an interesting, clearly written, and original reappraisal of received opinion on secularity and secularization in the modern West.'
Jeffrey L. Stout, Professor of Religion, Princeton University

A Short History
of Secularism

Graeme Smith

I.B. TAURIS

LONDON • NEW YORK

Published in 2008 by I.B.Tauris & Co Ltd
6 Salem Road, London W2 4BU
175 Fifth Avenue, New York NY 10010
www.ibtauris.com

In the United States of America and Canada distributed by
Palgrave Macmillan, a division of St. Martin's Press, 175 Fifth Avenue,
New York NY 10010

ISBN: (PB) 978 1 84511 577 7
ISBN: (HB) 978 1 84511 576 0

A full CIP record for this book is available from the British Library
A full CIP record is available from the Library of Congress

Library of Congress Catalog Card Number: available

Designed and Typeset by 4word Ltd, Bristol, UK
Printed and bound by TJ International Ltd, Padstow, Cornwall, UK

Contents

Acknowledgements

The bulk of this book was researched and written during a study leave granted by St Michael's College, Cardiff. I am very grateful to the Principal, Rev'd Dr Peter Sedgwick, for allowing me time to undertake the work.

I am fortunate to work in an environment which encourages exciting thoughts and new ideas. The staff and students of St Michael's College are great dialogue partners and I am constantly thankful for the chance to share their discussions. Peter Sedgwick, Stephen Roberts and Stephen Adams are excellent colleagues who have done much to develop my ideas. It is impossible to name all the students who should be thanked, but I hope they know they have taught me so much.

For the duration of the study leave, Luke Curran and Tina Franklin undertook the work which should have been mine. I very much appreciate their willingness to cover for me and I know I am lucky to have such wonderful colleagues. I am very grateful to them both for all that they do.

A number of people have read all or parts of the book. I must thank Manon Parry and Gordon Smith. Their comments were very helpful and guided me at each stage. Dr Angie Pears read the whole draft and offered insightful and supportive comments during the most important periods of the work. She is a very valuable and important friend who has done much to shape my thinking. I owe her an enormous debt of gratitude.

In Alex Wright I could not have wished for a better editor. He has been the inspiration and driving force behind the project. His analysis and comments have developed the work into its current form. It would have been a far worse book were it not for his efforts.

Of course, none of the above should be thought to agree with everything I say. The final conclusions and arguments are my own.

My partner Susannah has borne the brunt of caring for our family whilst I have worked on this book. She does this with her usual grace and intelligence. She has also read through sections and offered valuable critical comment from someone outside the theological academy. For this and for so much else I am exceptionally fortunate. It is with all my love that the book is dedicated to her.

Chapter One

Western Secularism

What does it mean to describe the West as secular? Does it mean that we are in the last days of Christianity? Is the Church facing inevitable and terminal decline? Has science and reason triumphed over superstition and myth in the culture of civilized peoples? Has the West progressed so far in its intellectual journey that it no longer needs the props and comforts of religion? Or is religion a strong and persistent facet of Western society? Is the twenty-first century, starting with that awful date 11 September 2001, to be the religious century? What are we to make of the fact that a majority in the West believe in God and tend to describe themselves as religious? It is after all a fact that, in a society which frequently describes itself as secular, a majority of people believe in God and call themselves Christian. The UK, which is often thought of as one of the more secular countries in Western Europe, illustrates the point. In its 2001 government-conducted census, 72 per cent of the population described themselves as Christian. In some regions, such as the North East and North West of England, this rose to an astonishing 80 per cent and 78 per cent, respectively. By contrast, 15.5 per cent stated they had no religion.[1] The data from the 1999/2000 *European Values*

Study reveals a similar picture across Europe. On average, 77 per cent of people stated that they believed in God. Those who called themselves a 'convinced atheist' registered at a mere 5 per cent, although a total of 28 per cent described themselves as 'not a religious person'.[2] And the figures for belief are higher for the USA. Such statistics are of course open to a variety of interpretations. For some the figures do not disprove the overall pattern of ongoing Christian decline, demonstrated by what they see as the more important and far lower numbers attending church services. They would argue that what people understand by Christian identity or belief in God is so vague as not to be meaningful. When comments about belief are made, what is intended is no more than a sense that they are good, decent people. For others the figures are evidence of a Christian persistence. They argue that ongoing belief in God requires an explanation. To say that religion is in decline is to miss an important part of the picture. Professor Grace Davie has argued that what the statistics show is that people have religious beliefs but they are not willing to belong to a church.[3] Regardless of whichever of the many interpretations is preferred, the difficulty remains. When we seek to describe contemporary secular Western society, then we need to take account of a persistent religious belief.

What I shall argue in this book, in very general terms, is that secularism is not the end of Christianity, nor is it a sign of the godless nature of the West. Rather, we should think of secularism as the latest expression of the Christian religion. What form does this new Christianity take? Secularism is Christian ethics shorn of its doctrine. It is the ongoing commitment to do good, understood in traditional Christian terms, without a concern for the technicalities of the teachings of the Church. Instead the desire to be and do good is supported by a sympathetic feeling towards the idea of God. In Western secular society we talk about good deeds, and on the whole we are charitable to our neighbours and those in need. But in public we do not talk much about Christianity. We can be generous and caring without at the same time needing to sort out the details of the doctrine of the atonement. Secularism in the West is a new manifestation of Christianity, but one that is not immediately obvious because it lacks the usual scaffolding we associate with the Christian religion.

Such an argument will not please those who think secularism is an ideology immersed in a life and death struggle with Christianity. For these secularists, who inhabit the rather polarized world of religious them and secular us, Christianity must be fought tooth and nail. The Church is a powerful enemy. It is deceitful and cunning, willing to employ all tactics necessary to maintain its elite status in society. Those who read this history and expect it to praise past secularists who nobly stood up for free thinking and scientific reason will be disappointed. However, neither does this book offer much comfort to the Church. Secularism is not presented here as the villain of the piece. Secularism has not corrupted Western society, leading its people away from the one true God into the false dawn of licentiousness and decadence. Secularism is not one of many sins, alongside materialism, consumerism and individualism, which demonstrate just how corrupt the West has become. In fact, throughout the book I challenge the sharp distinction between Church and world which the idea of secularism presupposes. Such a distinction is not at all helpful or even meaningful.

It is a commonplace to describe the West as a secular society. Religious leaders, journalists, sociologists, politicians and most people with a passing interest in its religious and cultural identity, both within and beyond its boundaries, assume the West is secular. Of course, exceptions are noted. Minority groups, especially immigrant communities, are recognized as having strong religious identities. But these exceptions are exceptions because of the assumption that the West is secular. One of three things is usually meant when the West is described as secular. The first, known as the secularization thesis, argues that institutional Christianity is in decline. The numbers of those attending Church Sunday by Sunday is down, as are membership figures. Fewer people turn to the

Church when they want to get married, baptize their children or bury their loved ones. Alongside the statistical decline is a loss of social status. Church leaders are rarely consulted as authoritative public voices. If they are, it is to talk about one limited topic, personal morality. So Bishops are asked about abortion, divorce or same-sex partnerships. However much this may frustrate Church leaders, who want to talk about poverty, the war in Iraq, conflict in Israel and Palestine or penal policies, the media consults them on matters of private behaviour. Studies show that the pattern of Church decline is not the same in each Western country. France differs from Italy, Sweden from Poland, and the USA is an exceptional case which needs special explanation, but generally the assumption is that the Church is coming to the end of its life. Sociologists and historians argue about the timing of the decline and about its causes, but these discussions do not affect the overall pattern. The Church as an institution is in meltdown.

The second way to describe the West as secular is to talk about the secularism of the public forum. By public forum. I mean the discussions and debates that often occur in the media, in schools and universities, and generally between people in the workplace and at home. These discussions are based upon secular assumptions. So religion is often treated as a matter of private opinion not public truth. Religious belief lacks the intellectual credibility of both natural and social science. There is a permitted relativism in private belief. It is sufficient to claim a religious belief as 'true for me' for it to be recognized as in some way valid. But the same does not apply to public truths such as scientific statements. The notion that the laws of gravity are a matter of private opinion, and therefore might be believed or not, rather than scientifically accepted public truth, is dismissed as nonsense in Western society. More controversially so is the idea that the earth and all living creatures were created in six days. The latter might be a matter of private belief, but the accepted normal view in the media is some form of evolution. The distinction between private religious beliefs and public truth and reason has led to the exclusion of theology, except in the small number of issues previously mentioned, from the media. Instead, public discussions are dominated by science. If there are technological advances, medical innovations or health benefits, then the predominant scientific voices are from the natural sciences. If the issues relate to society then sociological, economic or political voices predominate. This is the case even if the topic being discussed has obvious religious dimensions. One interesting illustration of the dominance of social scientific expertize was the reaction to the biographies of the London transport bombers of 7 July 2005. One of the bombers, the oldest member of the group, Mohammad Sidique Khan, was married, worked in a local primary school and community centre, and reportedly did not express controversial religious or political views in public. As such he appeared socially integrated. This left the media at something of a loss when it came to attributing reasons for his involvement in the attacks. Sociological reasoning could not provide a cause for his actions except to posit that the appearance of social integration was itself the deceit. Theological reasons were not deemed to be of themselves sufficient cause for his political alienation and consequent extreme violence. There was no expectation that a report on Khan's biography should begin with a discussion of his theology, because, until he participated in the bombings, this was a private matter. What this illustrates is the extent to which our public discussions are secular. They are based on assumptions which confine religious and theological matters to the private sphere, whilst shared public truths are scientific. The reasons for this development are often attributed to the rise of liberal philosophy and modern scientific method stemming from the Renaissance and Enlightenment. Important liberal and scientific Western thinkers, ironically themselves often faithful Christians, undermined the intellectual power of medieval Christianity.

The third way in which the West is described as secular is through the critical comments of religious bodies, not only the Church but also, importantly, Muslim theologians and leaders. The secularism of the West makes it the exception to global religious trends. To call the West secular is in part to make a comparative judgment. Christianity is a powerful cultural and political force in many countries in Africa, Latin America and Southeast Asia. Furthermore, Christianity is growing in these countries, not shrinking, albeit in markedly different forms from the West. In other African, Asian and Middle Eastern countries, Islam is a powerful force shaping cultural and political identity. What is interesting in terms of our analysis is that leading commentators from these religious groups, be it African Christians or Middle Eastern Muslims, share a common critique of the West. Those who condemn the social and cultural behaviour of the West bundle up a number of criticisms. These include, at its most extreme, Western secularism, alongside: militarism; imperialist capitalism; consumerism; personal moral breakdown; pornography; family neglect, especially of older generations; excessive and offensive liberalism; individualism; and materialism. Not all commentators equally condemn all aspects of Western society, nor are all those who condemn the West from outside its borders. Some Christian leaders and more conservative theologians in the West are also critical of its liberalism and its secularism. However, with varying degrees of venom, religious commentators describe the West as secular, something which is not regarded as a good thing.

In the next two chapters I shall investigate these three pictures of Western secularism in more detail. What should be noted here is the diverse range of people who describe the West as secular. In any study of society and culture, of Christianity and of global political relations, the designation of the West as secular is a common shared belief. It is the very assumed and commonplace nature of this description that makes secularism such an important subject for investigation. However, the description is far from unproblematic.

The study of contemporary secularism is the study of the religious and cultural identity of Western society. A number of options are available to the scholar wanting to pursue such an investigation. They might utilize sociological tools, and this has been done effectively by many, or cultural theories or historical analysis. These are all profitable ways of exploring the subject and have been employed successfully by many notable scholars. My intention in this book is wide-ranging. I wish to pursue a particular argument which explains the secularism of Western society. Therefore, aspects of different methodologies will be used for the study, including sociological analysis, historical work, cultural theory and, importantly, theological study. Throughout the study it will become clear how I have depended on the work of leading scholars in each field. It is by bringing the results of these different aspects of the study together that I hope to gain an accurate picture of the West's secular and religious identity.

There are four ideas which are central to my argument. They are: (i) Christianity has always been a religion with a fluid, evolving identity – it has a history of changing shape; (ii) medieval Christianity functioned in ways which are very similar to contemporary Western religion – the similarities are as striking as any differences; (iii) at the Enlightenment the major intellectual and cultural event was the separation of Christian ethics from Christian doctrine – and what is left is ethics practised in a Christian way; (iv) the Victorian era was an exceptional period of religious activity – it was by no means a normal time for the Church. I shall explain what is meant by these four ideas in more detail below. They are developed in response to the story that is normally told about the emergence of secularism. This starts with the premise that we can easily identify what Christianity actually is, that is, we know what not to believe anymore. If secularism is not Christian belief then there should be some sense of what this Christian belief is that is no longer believed.

The historical account of the emergence of secularism begins with the Middle Ages. The Middle Ages are seen as the golden era for Christianity, when all believed and went to Church. It is from this position that the Church has declined and society has become secular. The explanation for the decline of Christianity begins with the Enlightenment. During this period, atheism and anti-clericalism emerge as serious intellectual, social and cultural forces. The arrival of reason and science push religion out of the public square and into the realm of private opinion. That Christianity is in decline is confirmed by the statistics. The first important figures come from the Victorian era. All significant measures show that compared with the nineteenth century, the twentieth century has been a period of falling numbers. My argument challenges each of these aspects of secularism's traditional story in turn. Christianity is changing, often extremely rapidly, and has no permanent, static core. The religious activity of the Middle Ages was highly complex, by no means universally Christian and devout in any sense we would recognize today. It is in fact surprisingly similar to contemporary religious behaviour. At the Enlightenment there was a shift in the position of religion. What happened was not the triumph of atheism but instead the removal of doctrinal concerns from the public forum. This went alongside the persistence of ethics carried out on traditional Christian grounds.

Finally there has been institutional decline in Christianity since the Victorian era, but this should be understood in light of the exceptionally high levels of religious activity during the nineteenth century. What the figures show is not the decline of Christianity but its reversion to a normal status, something akin to what was happening during the Middle Ages, after the astonishingly high levels of Christianity displayed by the Victorians. The consequence of these historical processes is what might well be called the 'ethics society'. It is a society with an ongoing religious identity, in some ways very similar to the medieval period, a distinctive sympathy towards the idea of a God, conceived of in vaguely Christian terms, and an overriding concern with ethical issues. The ethics that this society practises are based on Christian premises. Such a society is of course contemporary Western society and it is what we now call secular. Whether the description has a long-term suitability is open to question. Also open to question is the capacity of the Church to respond to the new manifestation of its faith. However, before discussing these issues, the four central ideas need to be looked at in more detail.

The first proposal is that Christianity has always had a fluid and changing identity. What we think of now as Christianity is not the same as what would have been called Christian in the medieval period or during the days when the faith first came to Northern Europe. The question of Christian identity is a missionary question. It was as Christianity travelled, as it crossed national borders, that it changed. The social and cultural settings into which Christianity entered affected its beliefs and practices. This raised important questions. What elements of the faith belonged to specific local contexts, and might be jettisoned in alternative contexts, and what was permanent? What within Christianity was essential to the integrity and identity of the religion? Must you have the resurrection or the faith that Jesus is Lord or a commitment to a Church with a threefold order of bishops, priests and deacons? Most Christians want to insist that there must be an essential core of the faith to give it identity, although they do not agree on what that core would be. The problem for those who argue for an essential core is one of language and meaning. If there is an essential core of Christian belief which has a non-historical, static and discernible meaning, then there needs to be a way of talking about this core which can be understood by local people. It will be the context which will provide the cultural and linguistic tools necessary to make sense of the central beliefs and values. You cannot talk about the essential core of Christian belief, and be understood, without employing the local language. The local language is meaningful because of the social and cultural context in which it operates. So separating the essential core from the local is impossible because the core beliefs cannot be spoken about and heard without using local language. It is not possible to separate the ahistorical and transcendent from its immediate local expression. The consequence of this linguistic problem is that when the local cultural framework changes, so then does the essential core element which gives Christianity its identity. Christian identity is fluid because it changes whenever it enters a new context. As we shall see in Chapter Four the Church's history demonstrates this point repeatedly. At best each culturally and historical local church establishes afresh its view of what is meant by the core values of Christianity.

Equally problematic is the argument that Christianity has no core identity which is independent of a cultural and linguistic context. How can we talk of Christianity, and for that matter secularism, if it is impossible to identify what it is we mean? It cannot be the case that everything which claims to be Christian actually is Christian. There are too many diverse and opposing claims for this to be coherent. This does not mean that individual people and churches are not clear about what they think it means to be Christian or what is the essence of Christianity according to their theology. Rather, the confusion comes because there is no consensus amongst the competing and conflicting theologies and, perhaps more importantly, no consensus about what criteria exist to make decisions about the integrity of Christianity. The division between liberal and evangelical Christians over the issue of human sexuality is a contemporary illustration of this point. This discussion is rooted in vexed questions of biblical authority and interpretation, and this is only the tip of a very large iceberg.

At this point the dilemma of Christian identity is ecumenical. The ecumenical movement is the place where the Church has struggled with the question of how diverse Christianities can coexist without a destructive pursuit of theological or Church power and control. How can the churches survive without being dominated by what might be called a theological will to power? For some the very raising of questions of orthodoxy and heresy is itself illustrative of a fundamental error. The theological task is to assert the historical continuity of their version of the Christian tradition, usually by reference to biblical sources. For more liberal theologians the alternative position is to shift the discussion to questions of procedure and process. Christian identity is found in a willingness to cohabit with those with whom one cannot agree. It is conceded that agreement on matters of content is impossible. This means church communion is a methodological problem for those who wish to coexist and converse with doctrinal aliens. My examination of these issues will occupy Chapter Four.

The second idea to be examined is the notion that medieval Christianity functioned in ways which are very similar to contemporary Western religion. In Chapters Five and Six, I shall look at questions of medieval Christianity such as church attendance, the importance of the supernatural in everyday life and the extent of Christian belief. The assumption which underpins these chapters is that human beings are in some sense essentially religious and that the lived-out expression of their religion tends to be similar whether lived-out during the medieval period or today in the West.

The evidence we have of religious activity during the medieval period is incomplete. Many of the conclusions reached about medieval religious life depend upon sources which are difficult to read and interpret. We do not have the statistical data or sociological detail which informs our understanding of Christian practices and beliefs in the nineteenth and twentieth centuries. What we do have are historical records which throw up some illustrations of how medieval people behaved. Historians have then to make sense of the evidence as best they can. To do this they develop a story about the Church, Christianity and society which takes account of the existing historical data. The narrative which dominates historical accounts at the moment is that of high levels of medieval Christian belief and practice, certainly compared with the levels manifest in contemporary Western society. During the medieval period, Christian belief, especially belief in the supernatural, was the only intellectual idea with credibility. Church attendance was a common, if not quite universal, activity. Church leaders exerted political and social influence, especially through the instrument of excommunication. The contrast with Western secular society is all too apparent. So what has happened is that Christian belief and practice has declined since its medieval heyday.

Underpinning this story of medieval religious belief and practice is the assumption that everyone in medieval society was a religious activist. The only alternative to activism in the Middle Ages was heresy, and heresy led to excommunication and social and political exclusion, or worse. But such a picture seems unlikely. It suggests there must have been an enormous shift in human consciousness and behaviour between the medieval and the modern periods. Of course, some argue that the Enlightenment was such a shift. At the Enlightenment the intellectual atmosphere changed from the theological to the rational, scientific and technological. That the supernatural was no longer an effective explanatory tool demonstrates the changed mindset. The difficulty with this argument is that the current sociological data does not support it. A majority of people in contemporary Western society still believe in God, whatever they mean by this, and identify themselves as Christian. They have not abandoned the supernatural, nor, as Professor Steve Bruce, a leading advocate of the secularisation thesis points out, do they think or behave in especially rational ways:

> Increasing knowledge and maturity cannot explain the decline of religion. There are too many examples of modern people believing the most dreadful nonsense to suppose that people change from one set of beliefs to another just because the second lot are better ideas. The history of the human ability to believe very strongly in things that turn out not to be true suggests that whether something is true and whether it becomes widely accepted are two very different questions.[4]

In his book, Steve Bruce goes on to ask what sociological reasons can be given to explain the decline of Christian belief. I shall explore this in the discussion in the next chapter. However, there is a question to be asked prior to that about the decline of Christianity, which is: is decline the most accurate, valuable or informative analysis which can help us explain the contemporary religious landscape and account for the historical data?

An alternative account would be to argue that medieval religious behaviour is in fact very similar to that in the contemporary West. What we have today is minority Christian activism, the 15 per cent or so who attend church, alongside majority passive Christian support, the 70 per cent and more who claim some sort of Christian identity and express a vague support for the idea of a God. Medieval Christianity was the same. A minority were very serious about their Christianity, whilst a majority were supportive but from a distance. They did not want to make Christianity the centre of their lives, but nor did they want to challenge or abandon it. The majority have understood being Christian, whether in the contemporary or medieval period, as a matter of sharing a general sympathy for the beliefs and values of the Church. An important element of the sympathy towards the Church's values is the perception that the Church was a force for ethical conservatism. The role of the Church was, and is, to protect familiar social structures through its advocacy of conservative ethical behaviour, especially its emphasis on personal morality. An individual need not adhere to the Church's moral teaching to be glad that it exists and fulfils a conservative social function.

The notion of minority religious activism and majority support realigns Western Europe with the rest of the world. The narrative of Western European religious decline was simultaneously a story of its religious exceptionalism.[5] Nations outside of Western Europe, with the USA being the most controversial case, appear to be populated by large numbers of religious activists. The sociological story of Church decline had to explain what factors made Western Europeans essentially different from the rest of the world and, to confuse the picture, internally so variable in church attendance.[6] A narrative of minority activism and majority support begins from the straightforward notion that people are generally and essentially the same. They will of course be affected by social and cultural factors, but these will not produce a new, previously unrecognized *homo religio* or *homo non-religio*. Instead, what sociological factors explain is the balance between the minority activism and majority support, namely how large is the majority or how substantial the minority. Sociological factors will also explain the different types of passive majority support which exist throughout the world and, when the evidence in the medieval period is examined, the different types of majority support at different points in history. This is a far less difficult and ambitious task than seeking to explain why some countries in Western Europe are exceptionally secular. However, it leaves open the question of what did happen at the Enlightenment.

Apart from some occasional figures in classical antiquity, the traditional heroes of secularism lived during and after the eighteenth-century Enlightenment. It was at the Enlightenment that science and reason began its campaign against the fallacies and superstitions of religion. According to time-honoured historical accounts, everything changed at the Enlightenment: religion began its decline and secularism, especially atheism, moved to centre stage. There are, however, two problems with this version of history. First, atheism has never won anything but paltry support in the West. Second, Christianity was not removed from the public square. What happened was that doctrine ceased to be a topic of major concern, but ethics, and by this is meant Christian ethics, continued to dominate public discussion. So, and this is the third idea which shapes this book, at the Enlightenment what happened was not the success or even the beginning of the success of atheism, but the public transformation of Christianity from a religion of doctrinal orthodoxy to a religion of ethics.

One feature of contemporary Western secular society is the failure of atheism. The numbers of those who identify themselves as atheists or who belong to organizations such as the Secular Society or the American Humanist Association are extremely low. *The European Values Study* for 1999/2000 reported that on average 5 per cent of Europeans identified themselves as atheists. The country with by far the highest number of atheists was France with 15 per cent (the only country with more than 10 per cent), whilst many countries such as Britain, Austria, Italy, Greece, Finland and Russia reported numbers of 5 per cent or less.[7] What this means is clear. In the West people have not switched from Christianity to atheism. Insignificant numbers of people declare they do not believe in God. However, paradoxically, it does not mean that people see themselves as religious. In the same survey, 54 per cent of British people and a similar number of Swedes (7 per cent of whom described themselves as atheist) stated that they were not 'a religious person'. This drops to numbers in the 30s for countries such as Germany, Spain and the Netherlands, and is lower for many other European nations, the average being 28 per cent. Again we are faced by the problem of not being sure what people mean when they give these answers. They are probably not saying they are bad people, in contrast to the good folk who believe in God and think of themselves as Christian. What is likely is that they mean they are not committed to an institutional expression of religion, even though they do think of themselves as Christian. But this is speculation. What is apparent from the evidence is that whatever may have happened at the Enlightenment, it was not the start of the relentless march of atheism leading to a godless Western society. Given the statistical evidence, almost the opposite occurred; after the Enlightenment people affirmed their belief in God at least as much and possibly all the more.

If one feature of the Enlightenment is ongoing failure of atheism then a second is the continuing importance of Christianity. A number of political theorists and philosophers have argued that the ethics of the Enlightenment are based on Christian beliefs.[8] Historically this is a fact. Ideas of individual human worth and dignity, shared public reason, the progress of human society through history, and the ability of humanity to investigate its world, can all be traced to Christian theological sources. In some cases the foundational figures of liberal ideology and natural science were explicit about the Christian theological basis of their ideas. John Locke is a well-studied example. In other instances the pervasive presence of a Christian framework shaped the ideas which emerged during the Enlightenment. Individualism and human rights are classic examples of the ways in which Christianity provides the substantial ethic for public ideas. Still other Enlightenment thinkers did not expect there to be a clash between their ideas and their Christian faith; Immanuel Kant is the example oft cited here. It could be argued that whilst certain Enlightenment liberal and scientific ideas have their roots in Christianity, they have now travelled so far as to say they are no longer recognizably Christian. The Enlightenment began a process of change through which Christian notions were gradually separated from their theological origins to the point whereby they should no longer be called Christian. Any reply to this takes us back to the disputed territory of the identity of Christianity. It will depend on when the question of what is or is not to be counted as Christian gets fixed once and for all. It is apparent that I have argued that Christianity's identity has the fluidity and flexibility to accommodate the shifts being suggested here. This said, it is clear that some change did occur at the Enlightenment. We do not live in the same theological culture as the Middle Ages.

So what did change at the Enlightenment? To answer this we have to recognize what is missing from public debates after the Enlightenment. And the answer is 'doctrine'. Whilst contemporary ethics have a Christian heritage, it is equally the case that public discussions in Western society are not influenced by theology. The Church's debates about the nature of God, Christology, ecclesiology, the Bible, soteriology, salvation history and pneumatology do not concern sociologists, political theorists, economists, philosophers or cultural theorists. If there is explicit public interest in the Church's teaching, then it is usually around questions of personal sexual morality such as same-sex relationships, abortion, and divorce and re-marriage. What this absence of doctrine means for our history is that if public ethics is shaped by a Christian heritage then at some point in the West's history this was divorced from doctrinal questions. It has become possible to discuss an ethics derived from Christian belief without also discussing the doctrinal origins and implications of these beliefs. The point of that separation was the Enlightenment. Considered from the Church's perspective, it means that one of the missionary tasks in Western society is to decide the extent to which it is necessary or important to reconnect ethics and doctrine. This does not mean that the Church should seek to reclaim the Western ethical discourse as its own. Rather, it may mean that the Church has to recast its doctrine in light of the development of an ethics beyond its control.

The fourth and final idea to be examined states that the Victorian period was one of exceptionally high levels of religious belief and practice. This is central to our explanation of why contemporary sociology is dominated by the idea of Church decline. So far I have suggested that the religious activity of the medieval period was very similar to our own, a pattern of minority activism and majority support. The Enlightenment removed Christian doctrine from public discourses, but not from an identifiable Christian ethics. The question then is as follows: if our analysis is correct how do we account for the consensus amongst sociologists that the Church has by all measures declined? The notion of decline would seem to challenge the history I have so far presented. The answer to this question is twofold.

The notion of decline is a comparative notion. For there to be decline it must be from one thing to another. What this means is that you could have decline, but this decline might not be a sign that things are terminal, merely that they are returning to normal after an exceptionally high level. Decline might be a reversion to normal stable levels. This is what has happened with Christianity. The decline from the Victorian period to today is a decline, but one from an exceptionally high level to a more normal level. The exceptional religious activity of the Victorians reinforces the idea that contemporary

Christianity is in decline. Sociologists concur that measured against the Victorian era, Church membership, attendance and support is reduced. Horace Mann's national Census of Religious Worship of 1851 is taken to be the benchmark. Steve Bruce argues that 'about one-third of the British people attended church on the census Sunday in 1851'. Some put the figures higher, nearer 40–50 per cent of the population. By the 1980s this had declined to 'in Scotland 17 per cent of the population, in Wales 13 per cent, and in England 9 per cent'.[9] Other indicators such as clergy numbers and Church membership demonstrate a similar pattern of decline. It is notable that even at its peak, church attendance was not a universal activity. But this is not what reinforces the idea of decline. Rather, the demonstrable and dramatic indicators of diminishing support means that an assumption of decline achieves unquestionable status. In fact, as Bruce notes, the major dispute amongst sociologists and social historians is about the timing and causes of decline rather than its existence.

The nineteenth century was a period of exceptionally and uniquely high church attendance and support. The Victorian century was a Christian century like no other. It was an era of near equal Church activism and passive support. The widespread extent of Church activism meant that the public discourse was infused with Christian ideas and terminology. But the Victorian period was exceptional. It is no measure for contemporary religious belief and practice. Furthermore, its exceptionalism calls into question the idea of contemporary Church decline. The language of decline is entirely inappropriate to the contemporary Church. What would be better is the language of reversion. The Church has reverted to normal levels of religious belief and behaviour similar to the medieval period after the extremism of the Victorians. This is not necessarily of comfort to the churches, as they have an infrastructure to finance which depends on high levels of Church membership. The institution does not benefit from any reassurance that contemporary religious behaviour is not a condemnation of its practices. What it does do is make the Victorian era the oddity which requires explanation, not our own period and place. We may be less Christian than the Victorians, but they were far more Christian than anyone else.

I have in this long introduction set out the narrative which will guide this study. This has been necessary because this is not a straightforward history with a beginning, middle and end. Rather, I am using history, as well as social analysis and cultural theory, to understand the nature of contemporary Western secularism. My aim is as much popular and polemical as it is analytical. The discussion of my four central ideas form the basis of this history of secularism. It might seem that by focussing so much on the Christian religion I am doing a disservice to secular ideology's uniqueness and integrity. This is a danger. However, the focus on the paradoxical nature of contemporary belief as both Christian and secular recognizes not only the shared history of the two systems of thought, but also their joint importance for understanding the West's identity. It would not be possible to describe Western society as only secular without ignoring the significant religious indicators picked up regularly in surveys. Nor, however, can we describe the West as Christian – the picture is far more complex than that. It is by understanding the identity of Western society through a narrative which recognizes the interrelated strands of secular ideology and Christian theology that we achieve a history which makes sense of our contemporary religious, cultural and philosophical landscape.

Chapter Two

Science:
The New Technology

The purpose of this study is to deepen our understanding of the religious and cultural identity of Western secular society. As we embark on this study an obvious question arises: What is the problem with the historical accounts of secularism which already exist? This is the question that will occupy this chapter and the next.

The history of secularism has been told from one of two perspectives. One approach is to tell the story of secularism as social history. Secularism emerged in conjunction with modern society. The conditions of modern society, for example its urbanization, religious pluralism and social fragmentation, mitigated against religion's survival. Christianity declined because it could not survive modern life. We shall examine this account in the next chapter. The second perspective is to say that secularism won the battle of ideas. The emergence and development of secularism occurred because it was intellectually superior to Christianity and so convinced more people of its truth. In particular, science was able to marginalize Christian theology as an explanation for the way in which the world functioned. The Darwinian account of evolution and the Big Bang theory are intellectually more credible than the

Creation stories found in the book of Genesis. The intellectual conflict between secularism and religion will be the topic for this chapter.

This discussion begins with a critical examination of the traditional account of the emergence of secularism. There is one main problem with these accounts. Despite the triumph of science, religion has not subsequently disappeared. The USA is a good example of the dilemma. It is the most scientific nation in the world and yet religion remains an important, powerful social, cultural and political force. The considerable number of respected scientists who are also Christians is further evidence of the compatibility of science and Christianity. A history of secularism which focuses on the battle of ideas, especially between science and Christianity, has to explain the persistence of religion after the victory of science. What we shall see, somewhat surprisingly, is that it is the atheist Sigmund Freud who offers us clues to unravel this dilemma. He analyses how science has taken over religion's technological function. However, it is also apparent that religion has a key ethical function which science is not equipped to undertake. Hence Western society is technologically scientific but ethically it remains Christian. This will lead us to explore the notion that Western secular society should be thought of as the 'ethics society'.

The Traditional Account of the Rise of Secularism

If there is to be a founding father of secularism then it should be Anaxagoras. Anaxagoras was born in Clazomenae in Ionia around about the year 500 BCE.[1] He was invited to Athens by the ruler Pericles, as part of a project to educate the Athenians. As far as we know he lived there from 462 to 432 BCE. He is credited with introducing philosophy to the Athenians. He belonged to the scientific and rationalist tradition of Ionia and is believed to be the first who suggested the mind could be the cause of physical changes. Both Plato and Aristotle refer to his work. His claim to fame in secular circles derives from what he said about the sun and moon. As Pericles grew older and politically weaker, so his opponents began to attack him. This entailed attacks on his allies. Anaxagoras was accused of teaching heresy under new laws introduced by Athenians who had clearly had enough of being improved. What Anaxagoras taught was that the sun was not the god Helios making a daily pilgrimage across the sky, but in fact a red-hot burning stone. He also argued that the moon was made of earth and reflected the sun's light. For these irreligious ideas, Anaxagoras was persecuted. It is not clear exactly what happened after he was prosecuted except that Anaxagoras had to flee Athens, possibly with Pericles' help, and that he returned to Ionia. There he established a school.

What is it that qualifies Anaxagoras for founding father status? First and foremost it is that he refutes the supernatural explanation of the sun and moon and replaces them with a material, natural cause. It is doubtful that he could be described as a scientist by any modern definition. However, what gives him his status in secular history is the rejection of an otherworldly mythology. Second, he was persecuted for his scientific ideas by religious authorities. It might have been better had he been martyred, but even lacking this ideal (for all but Anaxagoras) he provided a good foretaste of what was to come. A feature of historical and contemporary secularism, as expressed by Western secular and humanist societies, is the sense that they are under constant threat from conservative religious forces. What happened to Anaxagoras later happened to Galileo and then Darwin.

The example of Anaxagoras is helpful because it illustrates what is generally meant when we seek to define secularism. Secularism is a way of thinking about the world and life which makes no reference to supernatural beliefs. Obviously this entails a rejection of religious beliefs. The world, and our life upon it, are to be examined, reflected upon and studied without reference to anything beyond what can be known by human beings here and now. It is a way of life or interpretation of life which only refers to the natural order, never the supernatural.[2] The question which traditional histories of secularism seek to answer is: How did we get from a world dominated by religious belief to one in which secularism, and especially science, were the most important means of understanding life?

Despite the existence of figures such as Anaxagoras, the real story of secularism begins after the Dark Ages. It starts with the first stirrings of the Renaissance and the onset of the end of the Middle Ages. This is the point when Christianity's intellectual dominance begins to be threatened. The first rival is humanism. For the new humanists the study of knowledge and the pursuit of wisdom can be undertaken without reference to the divine. Humanity can learn from one another and from the natural order. If people want to grow in knowledge and wisdom they can look horizontally at each other, the social sciences, and down at the ground, the natural sciences, rather than up to the heavens. The discovery of classical art, literature and philosophy opened the door to a humanist worldview. Other factors propelled the new trend forward. An increasingly prosperous middle class were more interested in the workings of commerce and economics than religion. The rise of nationalism produced another rival for affections previously directed towards the Church. Hard on the heels of the Renaissance came the Protestant Reformation. Economic, political and social forces combined with theological controversy to contribute to the disintegration of a monolithic Western Church. With theological divisions came a loss of Church authority. The Church no longer spoke with one voice. Local churches and sects clashed, often violently, undermining the influence each one might exercise. The religious wars following the Reformation encouraged many sensible people to abandon the divine in favour of the less bloody pursuit of human knowledge by and for the sake of humanity. None of this in itself meant secularism was the dominant intellectual force at the time of the Reformation; it clearly was not. But what had happened was that the unquestioned superiority of Christian theology, the Queen of the Sciences, was over.

Science came later and was initially no threat to Christianity. The first great scientists, Descartes, Kepler, Galileo and Newton, were religious men who did not imagine their ideas would eventually push God out of the public sphere. But as the eighteenth century developed and the rationalism of the Enlightenment took hold, so by gradual stages intellectual thought passed 'into deism, scepticism, and then with an easy step into atheism, for a God who is not needed to explain the present world was also thought not to be needed even as a "starter" of it.'[3] The Romantic era, the Methodist Revival, the Evangelical Movement and the rise of Pietism did nothing to halt the intellectual triumph of science and reason. As the nineteenth century progressed, new sciences such as biology, geology, anthropology, astronomy, eugenics and psychology further marginalized religion.

Two intellectual events encapsulate the capacity of science and reason to undermine Christianity. They both come from the nineteenth century. The first and most famous was the publication of Charles Darwin's *Origin of the Species*. As a result of Darwin's publication, human beings could explain their origins by and for themselves. They could do it in contradiction to the Church's account and, if they wished, without reference to the divine. If creation required a prime mover then this could be God, but such a God was hardly the personal, incarnate, miracle-performing God of the Church. Scientific study produced evidence to show the history of creation recorded in Genesis was wrong. The authority of the Church was duly diminished.

Less well-known but equally problematic for the Church was the advent of biblical criticism. Major books in the Old Testament were shown to be the amalgam of earlier source material. Stories, myths, legends and collections of wise words had been combined to produce the accounts in the Christian bible. A realization of the human part played in divine revelation increased accordingly. Textual researches into the New Testament revealed similar processes at work. Ultimately, fundamental questions would be asked about whether some sections of the Gospels previously treated as historical fact should still be regarded as such. For example, were the miracle stories meant to be treated as literal historical fact? Did Jesus say everything that was attributed to him? No one discovery or theory destroyed the truth of Christianity, but bit by bit its credibility was undermined. Science and reason seemed to know more about creation and revelation than the Church. Rufus Jones sums up the shift in human thinking over the course of four centuries: formerly the Church, with its 'inspired' scriptures, its 'ancient creeds', its priests, and its 'mysterious sacraments' had 'produced a spell on men's minds and had carried conviction against all opposition'. But now 'nothing could withstand the new authority of facts, of demonstration, of laboratory evidence'.[4]

The Church and Christianity were under assault from all sides. Enlightenment writers such as Voltaire could amusingly and pointedly ridicule the pretensions and pomposity of the French clergy, whilst Hume cast his sceptical eye over proofs for the existence of God. Nietzsche declared that God was dead, killed by humanity, and, more tellingly, Nietzsche trumpeted a will to power over the slave morality of Christianity. Feuerbach, a key influence on Marx, argued that God was a human construction, whilst Marx himself saw religion as a friend of the oppressor and a false comfort to the oppressed. The final nail in the Christian coffin came from Freud, who gave his scientific, psychological explanation for the advent of religion. It seemed that when humanity achieved good mental health, when it was fully grown up and mature, then religious beliefs could be cast aside like unwanted nursery toys. It had helped humanity in the infancy of its civilization, but now it was time to put away childish things.

There is a sense in which the detail of this historical account does not need to be true for the story to carry weight. The impression exists that intellectually secularism has won the battle. This is the case even though most people will not have studied Marx, Freud, Feuerbach, Darwin or Nietzsche and have only the vaguest notion of what they say. One aspect of Western society, a facet of its secularism, is that publicly Christian theology is no longer the source of all truth. Public debates, the media and conversations between friends and colleagues are not concerned with the doctrine of the atonement, a meaningful eschatology or developments in the idea of the Trinity. Rather, they are concerned with the social and natural sciences. They worry about health, criminal justice, the environment and economic security. Western secular society is one in which the formerly held dominant place of religion in the public sphere is over. But, and this is the important point, whilst the Christian religion no longer dominates Western society it has not been entirely removed from the picture. Christianity appears to have adapted so that it maintains an importance in Western society, whilst not being the only game in town.

The US Culture Wars

The example of the US culture wars illustrates the point I am making. Susan Jacoby, in her history of American secularism, reveals a shift in emphasis when thinking about secularism.[5] What is interesting for us is not so much the content of the book but the motivation for writing it, and the perception that Christianity is still a major political and cultural force in US society.

The hero of Jacoby's book is Robert Ingersoll, the renowned 'Great Agnostic'. Ingersoll was a nineteenth-century speaker who dabbled in politics before becoming famous for his amusing, engaging attacks on the Church. The son of a Presbyterian minister (inevitably) Ingersoll, toured the USA – speaking in public and advocating a humanist alternative to Christianity. He sought to liberate people from the restrictions of religion and offer them a vision of humanity freely pursuing a reasoned way of life for the good of society. For Ingersoll religion was a prison which incarcerated people in superstition and prevented them from realizing their true nature. Jacoby quotes from one of his speeches:

> We are laying the foundations of the grand temple of
> the future – not the temple of all the gods, but of all
> the people – wherein, with appropriate rites, will be
> celebrated the religion of Humanity. We are doing what
> little we can to hasten the coming of the day when
> society shall cease producing millionaires and
> mendicants – gorged indolence and famished industry –
> truth in rags, and superstition robed and crowned.
> We are looking for the time when the useful shall be
> honourable; and when REASON, throned upon the
> world's brain, shall be King of Kings, and God of Gods.[6]

Some of the sense of the passage is lost to the rhetorical effect. What is apparent, however, is the intention to promote and celebrate the possibilities of humanity freed from religious belief. The main emphasis is an attack on the pernicious effects of religion.

The shift of emphasis is illustrated by Jacoby herself. The purpose of her history is to remind the American public of its honourable humanist heritage, the unambiguous freethinking of the book's title. The reason this is necessary is the major threat posed to basic freedoms by the Christian right. Jacoby is taking up arms in the culture wars which pervade US politics. She fears for the stranglehold the Christian right has over the Republican Party. She despairs that Al Gore, the Democratic candidate, stated during the 2000 presidential campaign that he would ask himself 'What would Jesus do?' prior to major executive decisions. She believes that the American public sleeps whilst the essential and fundamental separation of Church and state is gradually eroded. In fact, this complacency, the 'unexamined assumption' that 'religion per se is, and always must be, a benign influence on society', is an 'indispensable condition for the successes of the ultraconservative minority'. Jacoby's mission is to awaken the US public to the dangers of renewed religious influence and power. A major weapon in Jacoby's retaliatory armoury is to equate the Church with social conservatism and humanism with social reform. The rise of the feminist movement is an oft-cited example. Humanists such as Ingersoll have long supported the movement for women's rights, whilst the Church has defended the status quo. The issue of abortion is another example. In fact, the only exception is the Civil Rights movement and the role played by the Black Churches in supporting equal rights. Usually, Jacoby argues, the Church resists social change.

Jacoby's work is illustrative of the new priorities which pervade secularism. Arguments about the existence of God and the relationship between reason and faith have been relegated to the lower division of humanist concerns. Writers such as Richard Dawkins, who wish to end public support for Christianity, make little impact on popular belief despite their high media profile. Their issues are yesterday's news and their fights marginal skirmishes. Such a statement might seem surprising. So often a subject like evolution appears to be the central topic around which scientists and Christians gather to differ. It grabs all the headlines, especially in the USA. Schools have become the battleground. Christian groups are arguing that Darwin's theory of evolution is just that, a theory, and so should not be taught in schools either as fact or as superior to the Genesis account. They argue that the evidence for evolution is partial and flawed. Frequently, to the annoyance of scientists, they quote those who agree with evolution to illustrate their beliefs, including Darwin himself. The scientists claim, usually correctly, that they have been quoted out of context or were making rhetorical points. The pro-evolutionists, with Professor Richard Dawkins at the vanguard, argue that the scientific evidence overwhelmingly supports Darwin's analysis.[7] So it would seem that the creationism versus evolution debate is the obvious place to begin an analysis of the clash between secular science and Christianity, not least because this is a point at which science and Christianity seem to come into direct conflict.

But we shall not be focusing on this issue, because a majority of Christians are very happy to accept Darwin's theory of evolution. It is not a moment of belief or unbelief for Western Christians. Nor is it perceived as the major threat confronting secularists. It was a serious public issue in the nineteenth century, but Christianity has moved on since then and accommodated this and many other advances in scientific knowledge. This is not to deny it is a cause célèbre for certain evangelical Christian groups in the USA. They work hard to make it a state and national issue. However, effective political agitation by some evangelical Christians does not mean creationism is important or illustrative for an analysis of Western society. The question of the origins of the Earth could, one imagines, be 'solved' with only minimal impact on either attendance at church or the intellectual credibility of Christianity. If Genesis were shown to be correct, then it is unlikely the masses would start going to Church. Likewise if Darwin, or modern neo-Darwinians such as Dawkins, were finally proven right beyond all possible doubt, it is improbable that those currently belonging to the Church would blanche and exit. At its most significant it is a problem of education and religious freedom, in itself an important issue, but not the most important for the relationship between science and Christianity.

What this adds up to is a truce between science, reason and religion. The more immediate worry for secularists is the resurgence of religion in the political sphere. The USA is the major source of concern. In the USA, Christianity is a major social and political force. Christianity has clearly not gone away.

The political situation for Western Europe is more complex. The attention of the media has been more on Islam. This can range from arguments about the wearing of the veil in France and the UK to radical, militant clerics inciting violence and hatred against Israel and the USA. The terrorist attacks in London and Madrid make it clear that religious belief is important in the West. But this is religion from outside of the West's cultural and intellectual heritage. This is not to say that Islam is not a present and current part of Western European cultural and religious identity. It also has an important place in the history of many Western European countries such as Spain and Turkey, to name but two. Furthermore, those who carried out the attacks in London were British Muslims integrated into British society. But, and this is the important distinction, the history of secularism in the West is the history of its relationship with Christianity. Those who argue that secularism has usurped religion in the West are arguing that the religion being replaced is Christianity, not Islam. It may be that in the future we need also to talk about the way in which Western society has undermined Islam in the lives of Western European Muslims. But we are not there yet. Interestingly, this is a point made by Muslim scholars. Azzam Tamimi argues that secularism is a product of Christian society. What he calls 'Arab secularism' arose in very different social and cultural conditions.[8]

The question arises as to whether anything similar to the US culture wars is occurring in Western Europe. The simple answer to this is 'no'. Issues such as abortion, legalized same-sex marriage and evolution do not have the same political status in Western Europe as they do in the USA. Nor are Western European politicians required to be explicit about their commitment to the Christian faith in the same way as US candidates. But there are signs that some politicians in Western Europe would like to stress a Christian heritage. This can range from comments about the Christian history of Europe put in the draft European Union Constitution to the exploitation of identity fears by parties such as the British National Party. The latter argue they are protecting British identity when they advocate Christian values, although some see this as a code for attacks on Muslim communities. If this trend continues then it may well be that a different form of culture wars will emerge in Western Europe. The polarities will be radical fundamentalism and liberal rights to tolerance and freedom. Different versions of Christianity and Islam may well position themselves in different places on this spectrum. But this is speculation based on weak signs of an emerging cultural conflict in Western Europe.

We are left with two problems which call into question the traditional account of the emergence of secularism in the

West. The first is that clearly Christianity has not gone away. In the USA in particular, Christianity continues to be of major political importance, especially when employed to support socially conservative movements. The second is that, despite the apparent intellectual superiority of secular ideas over Christianity, and the rise of the natural and social sciences, intelligent people are still becoming Christians. Not least, respected and established scientists are practising Christians and some write books on the compatibility of their faith and academic work. If secularism has won a major victory then somehow Christianity appears to have changed the rules of the game. These two problems require us to revise the traditional account of the history of secularism.

Sigmund Freud and The Future of an Illusion

The major clues to how we should understand the identity of Western secular society come from the work of Sigmund Freud. Freud highlights two fundamental points. First, he shows how science became Western society's new technology. Science replaced the technological function of Christianity. Science was better at explaining natural phenomena. Second, science could not provide an ethical framework for Western society, so religion remains in the West as a tool for ethical decision making.

Freud was a committed scientist. As the founding father of a new discipline, his scientific credibility was viewed sceptically by established scholars. Peter Gay describes in some detail throughout his biography how Freud struggled with his marginal status.[9] But this did not prevent Freud from extolling his own approach as scientific. The fear of derision probably encouraged Freud to be something of the arch-scientist.

Freud believed that science could explain and, more impressively, allow humanity to control the natural order. He wrote: 'We believe that it is possible for scientific work to gain some knowledge about the reality of the world, by means of which we can increase our power and in accordance with which we can arrange our life. If this belief is an illusion, then we are in the same position as you.'[10] The 'you' in this sentence refers to religious believers. The quotation comes from the end of Freud's book on religious belief, *The Future of an Illusion*. Freud's clear conviction, spelt out in the book, is that science is no illusion. Science has the capacity to explain reality and then equip humanity to control it. It does this better than religion. In fact, science can explain the persistence of religion after the emergence of science.

Freud begins his analysis of religion by asking why it is that we accept the restrictions imposed by civilization. In particular, why do we accept the moral limitations that come with living in society? For example, successful participation in social life means we do not murder those who annoy us nor steal another's possessions because they are attractive. The answer Freud gives is that it is better than the alternative. Living in civilized society is preferable to a life threatened by 'nature'. Freud is quite dramatic in his language here. Nature, he says, 'destroys us'. It does this 'coldly, cruelly, relentlessly' and, as if to emphasize the cruelty, sometimes 'through the very things that occasioned our satisfaction'. Civilization is the mechanism humanity has developed to defend itself from nature. This is not merely a defence against the physical dangers of the natural world. It is also a psychological defence against life's random, arbitrary brutality. As Freud says, civilization's task is manifold and multi-faceted. Humanity's 'self-regard, seriously menaced, calls for consolation; life and the universe must be robbed of its terrors; moreover his curiosity, moved, it is true, by the strongest practical interest, demands an answer'.[11] Civilization, through its culture and religion, is required to explain all aspects of humanity's life including the very purpose of that life.

The first stage by which nature is robbed of its terrors and life's mysteries are unravelled is for people to humanize nature. Death and disaster are understood to be the product of a malignant or maligned ill will. The natural elements have all too human emotions that can rage, soothe or enchant us.

Humanity can comprehend nature as a reflection of its own characteristics. And this means, Freud argues, that we can understand nature by seeking to engage with the personalities we turn it into. Confronted with nature's characters, 'we can try to adjure them, to appease them, to bribe them, and, by so influencing them, we may rob them of part of their power'. The endowing of nature with personality offers humanity the possibility of reducing the outright terror and bewilderment it might otherwise feel.

This is but the first stage. Humanity does not stop at endowing nature with personality and will. There is a second stage. Humanity reaches back into its own early experiences of fear and protection. There it comes across the parental figure and, especially, the father. Freud writes that 'man makes the forces of nature not simply into persons with whom he can associate as he would his equals – that would not do justice to the overpowering impression those forces make on him – but he gives them the character of a father'.[12] And when the personalized nature adopts the father identity it becomes divine. Humanity turns personalized nature into the gods. For 'gods' are the expression of the father memory in the character of nature. These gods have a threefold task: to 'exorcise the terrors of nature'; to reconcile people to the 'cruelty of Fate'; and to 'compensate them for the sufferings and privations which a civilized life in common has imposed on them'.

Nor is this the end of the story. The best of humanity, 'the most gifted people of antiquity', realized that of the three tasks the one the gods excelled at was the third – compensation for the misfortunes of life. As human knowledge and understanding grew, so it appeared that the gods' participation in nature was limited. The gods might still be in overall control of nature but they rarely seemed to get involved in its daily events. Nature was autonomous. It had a destiny all of its own, and to which on occasion the gods themselves might be subject. So people began to focus on the role of the gods in civilization and in particular to home in on the area of morality. Freud argued: 'the more autonomous nature became and the more the gods withdrew from it, the more earnestly were all expectations directed to the third function of the gods – the more did morality become their true domain'.[13] The role of the gods was to improve the operations of civilized society so that it might be more just and the suffering inflicted by humans on each other reduced. It was to 'watch over the fulfilment of the precepts of civilization' which human beings 'obey so imperfectly'. The triumph of religion was ethical. Moral laws were written into the fabric of reality by their elevation to a divine origin and legitimization. Morality was more than a means of ordering human civilization; it was a universal and eternal truth about life and nature.

Freud had now laid the foundations for his description of contemporary religious life. Religion fulfils a psychological function. It makes our fear and helplessness tolerable by protecting us against cruel fate and human injustice. Religion provides an explanation of reality which need not fill us with terror or lead to despair. Life has a purpose beyond what is immediately observable and experienced. There is a higher order above the human and there are benevolent personalities ensuring our fates are not arbitrary. Once these psychological foundations are laid, Freud seems to believe that human imagination can construct religious systems which are ever more refined and satisfying. An important progression is life after death. He writes that in the end 'all good is rewarded and all evil punished, if not actually in this form of life then in the later existences that begin after death. In this way all the terrors, the sufferings and the hardships of life are destined to be obliterated. Life after death, which continues life on earth just as the invisible part of the spectrum joins on to the visible part, brings us all the perfection that we may perhaps have missed here'.[14] It was but a small step to compress all the attributes of the gods into one divine figure. The great advance to monotheism was simultaneously a return to the origins of religion as human relations with the one God could now more precisely mirror the intimacy of relations with the father.

So it is that Freud creates an explanation of Western Christian beliefs. Religion is an illusion. It is not a delusion because it does not necessarily contradict reality. Illusions may be true and as yet merely not proven. For Freud, technically religion is neither proven nor falsified, although he is most autobiographical when he speaks as an atheist. What makes Freud suspicious of religion, and what makes it an illusion, is the key part played by 'wish fulfilment'. Religion offers humanity what it most desires. Life is just, ordered and meaningful because there is a God who is benevolent, fair and in control of nature. Religion shelters humanity from the bleak, cruel, random, pointless suffering inflicted by nature. For Freud it will only be when humanity grows up, when it shakes off its dependence on fatherly protection and security, that religion will cease to be part of civilization.

What are we to make of Freud's scientific analysis of religion? By his own omission Freud was not happy with *The Future of an Illusion*. He called it 'childish' and 'feeble analytically, inadequate as self-confession'. To his friend and colleague Max Eitingon, he criticized the book, saying 'the analytic content of the work is very thin' and adding that 'it is not worth very much'.[15] Peter Gay attributes Freud's self-criticism in part to the regular depression and defensiveness he felt on publication of his work. But he also noted that the criticism was more severe and vehement than usual. Gay thinks that Freud was feeling both old and battered, not least because of the effects of his cancer. This may be true – it is an ongoing theme in Gay's biography – but it is not the only reason for Freud's despondency with the work.

The Future of an Illusion is a very different type of book from Freud's early classic works. The earlier lectures and books on dreams and hysteria are based on Freud's work as a therapist. He employs evidence from individual cases to support the conclusions he draws and the theories he devises. People came to him with discernible, observable problems. As a result of conversations in which Freud was able to employ strategies based on his theoretical analysis, the presenting symptoms frequently reduced or disappeared. In this sense Freud could properly call himself a scientist. That others have equally observed changed behaviour and as a result either agreed with Freud's theories, developed them, or, like Jung, challenged them, adds weight to the scientific label. There are reported, observable cases subject to forms of verification. What is apparent is that none of this is the case when Freud changes tack and starts to write about society. Gay suggests Freud brings the tools of psychoanalysis to his study of civilization. But such an assertion seems improbable. Freud cannot psychoanalyse Western society as he would a patient. It is not clear if Freud believed Western society displayed symptoms in need of treatment. Religious behaviour would need to be a form of mass hysteria or neurosis which endangered the social order. Freud himself did not claim this much. Religion is an illusion not a delusion. Religion may or may not be true, it is not proven, even though Freud the atheist did not himself believe.

Furthermore, Freud's speculation about the relationship between monotheism and an adult's memory of the childhood image of the father is not based on the psychoanalysis of religious believers. Freud had not carried out the qualitative empirical work. Nor, it should be noted, do religious people display behaviour of sufficiently similar type to suggest they could be classified as one group with one observable set of personality disorders. Religious believers are diverse in personality type, character and individual behaviour. It might be argued that Freud's work on *Totem and Taboo* provides the evidence for the relationship between the human manufacture of the gods and their childhood memories of the father. Freud refers to the earlier work in a footnote in *The Future of an Illusion*. However, such a claim would be more than Freud intended. He stated that the purpose of *Totem and Taboo* was not 'to explain the origin of religions but only of totemism'.[16] And, whilst there are connections between Freud's speculations in *The Future of an Illusion* and his work in *Totem and Taboo*, it is the case that they discuss essentially different topics. In *The Future of an Illusion*, Freud has moved away from the scientific methodology which served him so well in his psychoanalytic work and entered the realm of speculation.

But Freud's work is not important to us because of its ability to analyse why humans engage in religious behaviour. Rather, Freud highlights two significant and interrelated points which are key to understanding the religious identity of Western society. The first is the straightforward point that Freud makes, namely that the value of religion to contemporary civilization is in its capacity to support ethical systems. Freud is correct in arguing that at the heart of the West's religion is ethics. But (and this is the second point) Freud is wrong about the reasons for the West's religion of ethics. Freud recognizes that the relationship between nature and religion is key to understanding religion's importance in a society. Furthermore, Freud is correct in arguing that one of the roles of religious belief is to exercise control over the dangerous and terrifying natural order. This is what is meant by religion exercising a technological function. There is much historical evidence to support the idea that religion functioned in this way. Where Freud struggles is in his attempt to argue that science and religion are of a different intellectual order, the one a means of establishing the truth and the other an illusion. In fact, what has happened historically is that science has merely replaced religious belief as the most effective technology at humanity's disposal. Science in one sense is the new religion – because of its technological prowess. The big difference is that science is a technological system that requires someone else to do the ethics. Whereas religion provided its own ethical framework, science comes equipped only with the limitations that humans wish to impose on it. So if science is Western society's source of technology, then it needs to be simultaneously developing a public conversation about ethics. This is the value of Freud's work. Its implications need to be examined in more detail.

The New Technology

This book is not a history of the relationship between science and religion, but there is one important point we need to take from that history to help us understand contemporary religious identity and in particular the nature of Western secularism. Science has replaced religion as the technology of Western society. The important role that religion played in ancient and medieval society was technological. It was by no means the only role it played, but it was highly significant. An example from history illustrates what I mean.

Science's greatest public success has been in the field of health care. Prior to science, Christianity was the most effective medical remedy for illness and disease. It had replaced paganism as the most effective source of medical cures. Professor Peter Brown, in his monumental biography of Augustine of Hippo, sums up the technological function of religion, in particular Christianity, in ancient medicine. Of the religious culture of fourth century CE, he writes:

> Augustine grew up in an age where men thought that they shared the physical world with malevolent demons. They felt this quite as intensely as we feel the presence of myriads of dangerous bacteria. The 'name of Christ' was applied to Christians like a vaccination. It was the only guarantee of safety. As a child, Augustine had been 'salted' to keep out the demons; when he had suddenly fallen ill, as a boy, he would plead to be baptized. These Christian rites of course, might influence a grown-up man's conduct as little as the possession of a certificate of vaccination; but they expressed a mentality that had cut off, as positively 'unhygienic', the pagan religion of the classical past.[17]

It is possible of course to be highly sceptical about these religious practices. They can be dismissed as superstition. The notion that Christ was the most effective weapon against demons might be biblical but it is not modern, medical or scientific. But that would be to do a major injustice to the intellect and culture of our forebears. Good health and long life are no more important now than they were in times past. Those living at the time of Augustine were as enthusiastic for what worked as we are today, and equally as dismissive of what failed. So there is a sense in which Christianity was the best medicine. It would not have been perfect, but then modern medicine does not cure every disease. This does not stop contemporary people from investing their faith in the ability of modern medicine to cure illness. Likewise, the ancients hoped for the best from their Christian faith. For hundreds of years Christianity was seen as the means to ensuring prosperity and good health. It was only with the emergence of modern medicine that this technological function ceased. And it is perhaps ironic that many of the temples to the new scientific technology, hospitals, were established by Christian benefactors. This said, it also shows the adaptability of the Christian religion.

With the emergence of science as the new technology, a new problem arose. Before science's triumph the gods had limited what might be technologically possible. The will of the Divine had set boundaries on how the technology would function. These boundaries were set by the permissions granted by the Divine. But, once the supernatural had been usurped, then the restrictions on human possibility were also lifted. What was possible was now a matter of human choice, invention and imagination rather than divine permission. The question for technology was no longer what was allowed by the supernatural. That question had been answered, at least in theory, in as much as anything was possible. All that had to happen was that it had to be invented. In practice this might be a major qualification, but in theory it was no boundary at all. This infinite possibility brought with it a new question. Was what was possible also desirable? That something could be done did not mean it should be done. The issue of abortion is a clear illustration of this point. It is possible for a fetus to be aborted if the parents so wish. The science permits this. But it is a very different question to ask whether this should be done. The science had generated a set of questions about the desirable which were free from supernatural restriction. In other words, Western society now had to find new ways of dealing with ethical questions in light of the technological dominance of science. Or it had to revise the old ways, namely Christianity. The consequence of science becoming the new technology was the emergence and dominance of ethics as the most important discussion topic in the West. Ethics was the main dilemma facing a society which had broken the shackles of religious technology. As discussed later in this book, the religious shift to ethics was a major defining factor for Western secular society. What is notable is that, in the absence of a scientific ethical system, Christian ethics remain firmly in place. The choice for Western society was between Christian ethics or no ethics.

It is at this point that we understand the meaning of the US culture wars. They are US society battling out the territory occupied by ethics. On the one side is the social conservatism associated with Christian ethics; on the other is a secular liberalism which is pro same-sex marriage, pro a woman's right to choose and pro-science. Both sides of the argument are a version of Christian ethics, albeit versions that have followed very different trajectories. What makes the fighting so vicious is that it is an internal theological dispute – a Christian civil war. What I mean here will be clarified in the final chapter. At this stage in the argument my point is that the US culture wars are a further illustration of how science is unable to remove religion from its role as ethical arbitrator and guide.

I began this chapter with a traditional account of the rise of secularism. In the battle of ideas between naturalism and supernaturalism it is the sciences which have come out on top. In the public sphere it is the natural and social sciences which have credibility. At best, religious belief is a matter of private opinion. Telling this traditional story has highlighted two problems. They evolve around the persistence of religion despite the supposed victory of secular ideas. First, Christianity plays a vital part in the high-profile cultural wars being played out in US politics. Second, most Christians are able to combine their faith with scientific knowledge and, in some cases, extensive expertise. These difficulties required a different account of the conflict between secularism, and science in particular, and Christianity. In the revised account I argued that science has replaced religion as the effective technology in Western society. Science is functionally superior to religion and provides better explanations of the working of nature and human life. However, science has not so far developed an adequate ethical system. Hence in the field of ethics it has not been able to displace Christianity. In the chapter on the Enlightenment, I shall explore this argument in more detail. However, before that we must look at the second of our traditional accounts of the history of secularism, namely the social history.

Chapter Three

Secularism and Social History

The second and more common way to discuss the emergence of secularism in the West is through the medium of social history. At the heart of the discussion is the much debated secularization thesis. The contemporary form of the theory was developed during the 1960s and 1970s by scholars such as Peter Berger and Bryan Wilson, although it could be claimed it stretches back to the nineteenth century and such influential figures as Marx, Durkheim and Comte.[1] The more recent, authoritative and trenchant exponent of the thesis is Professor Steve Bruce. In essence what is argued is that Christianity has declined because of social change. Secularization can be explained by the modernization of Western society. The capacity of Christianity to defend its intellectual credibility against the inroads of secular ideas is less important than its ability to withstand social change. As society became more industrial and urban and therefore socially fragmented and bureaucratic, so Christianity became less popular and more marginal. In fact, Steve Bruce has predicted that 'Britain in 2030 will be a secular society'.[2] Bruce is almost certainly mistaken in his prediction, for reasons that will become apparent as the chapter progresses. But it is clear that social change has had a significant impact on Christianity and the Church. It is this impact that I shall investigate here.

The chapter begins with a presentation of the commonly used statistics of Church decline, which are relatively uncontroversial. Next is an exploration of the different explanations of Western secularization. Bruce's theories of modernization, in particular social fragmentation, the end of community and technical rationality, are the starting point for the investigation. Bruce's explanation has been challenged by a number of scholars. It has been argued that what he explains is the decline of the Church, but that this is different from decline in Christian belief. Allied to this is the claim that he has a very narrow notion of what constitutes Christian belief and practice. The modernization thesis also has to take account of the situation in the USA, where the statistics for Christian belief and church affiliation are far more robust. A further set of questions comes from the work of Callum Brown. He argues that the major decline in Church life began during the 1960s and is a product of the last 40 years. The explanation Brown favours concerns the changing identity of women. It has little to do with the industrialization or urbanization of Western society. Finally, I shall look at the notion of vicarious religion put forward by Professor Grace Davie. This, allied with ideas of popular religion, questions the extent to which Christianity is in retreat in Western society.

The Statistics of Decline

The argument that Western society is becoming more secular begins with statistics. It is usually undisputed that across a range of indicators contemporary support for the Church is declining compared with the nineteenth century. The pattern is not uniform across Western society. The USA is an exception which requires detailed investigation. Nor are all countries in Western Europe the same. Reported attendance at religious worship is higher in Portugal and Ireland than it is in France or Sweden.[3] These variations can be attributed to the different

religious cultures of these countries and regions and also to
the political history of the nation state. The Roman
Catholicism of Ireland and the anti-clericalism of France illustrate how local and national factors will impact on the overall
picture. However, the local variations do not disprove the overall pattern of decline in church affiliation and attendance.
With the exception of the USA, which is considered below,
there is no Western country that challenges the trend of
Church decline. There is no space here to consider all nations
and regions of Western Europe, and so I shall follow Bruce and
look in detail at the UK. The UK is a good example of how the
social explanation of the rise of secularism is presented.

Across all indicators the contemporary statistics for
Christian belief and behaviour show a pattern of decline.[4] In
1851, when Horace Mann conducted his national Census
of Religious Worship, somewhere between 40 and 60 per cent
of the population of the UK attended church. The precise
number is hard to estimate because of the number of people
who attended more than once on a Sunday, but we can reasonably assume that no less than 40 per cent of the population was
in church. In 1979 the figure was 12 per cent, it was 10 per cent
by 1989 and less than 8 per cent by 1999. This is a huge decline
and reveals a major shift in religious behaviour. Other indicators reveal the same pattern. The number of clergy fell by
about 25 per cent between 1900, when there were 45,400, and
the year 2000, when there were 34,160. During the same
period the UK population nearly doubled, so if clergy numbers
had kept up there should now be nearer 80,000. In 1900 about
50 per cent of children attended Sunday School, whereas by
1998 the number was 4 per cent. The number of marriages
conducted in church halved during the twentieth century from
about 80 per cent at the start to less than 40 per cent
by the end. There have also been substantial reductions in
the number of newly born children being baptized and the
number of funerals conducted in church. The conclusion to be
drawn from this data, and it is uncontested, is that compared
with the nineteenth century there is far less support for the

Church. There is disagreement about the detail of Church decline, with Brown arguing that the 1960s were the key period of social change, but about the overall pattern there is little dispute. We are far less committed to our churches than the Victorians. The question which naturally follows is: How do we explain this decline?

Modernization

Steve Bruce argues that decline in church affiliation and attendance can be explained by the changes which accompany the emergence of modern society.[5] There are three factors in particular: social fragmentation; the end of community; and rationalization. I shall examine each of these factors in turn.

The first shift in social conditions that Bruce identifies is the shift from tightly knit, closed communities, the villages, to diverse fragmented society, the contemporary nation state. This fragmentation had a number of elements. In pre-modern, feudal communities, the Church would have responsibility for a number of key activities. It would be responsible for education, social welfare and heath care, and it would have influential opinions on the operation of economics. With the advent of modernization these activities progressively became the remit of specialists. The Church lost overall control. Trained professionals such as teachers, nurses, doctors and social workers took over responsibility for work that had previously been the responsibility of the Church. If the Church retained management of an institution, for example a school or social welfare organization, the professional standards exercised by the organization meant it was identical to a secular body. A Church-run school would still employ teachers with the same professional qualifications as a state-run school. To all intents and purposes it would be the same.

Alongside the fragmentation of roles people started to separate into more distinct class groups. In the feudal era divisions in society were fixed and well recognized. However, despite the divisions servant and master tended to inhabit the same social and physical space. Whist the quality of life for some was far better than for others, nevertheless all lived in close proximity to each other. With the advent of urbanization and industrialization, society began to fragment. Different classes of people would work in different places; notably the working classes would fill the factory shop floor. Class distinction would also impact on living spaces. Again the working classes would congregate together in vast urban slums, whilst the wealthier either moved out of the city altogether or moved away from the centre to the edges. As suburban housing developed it was populated by the middle classes.

These social changes affected the mindsets of populations. Industrialization led to the breakdown of the feudal system and thereby introduced a greater sense of egalitarianism and democracy. Bruce argues that this impacts on the Church, which finds it harder to defend the feudal notion of episcopal hierarchy. So a strongly episcopal church such as the Church of England continues to hold the aristocracy and gentry, whilst Protestant Nonconformist churches, with their more democratic structures, appeal to the new middle classes. The changed mindset is central to Bruce's analysis. The breakdown of the rigid and hierarchical feudal society, in which the Church had a dominant and powerful role, creates a social fragmentation which goes hand in hand with an individualism finding lasting expression in egalitarianism.

Implied within the social fragmentation is the second condition of modernization, namely the breakdown of community. Again the starting point is a picture of medieval life dominated by small and close-knit communities. The key feature of these communities was an absence of pluralism. Their belief systems were not open to external challenge and thereby had a 'taken for granted' status. In the absence of alternative theologies, religious beliefs were treated as facts. They were beyond the realm of questioning. Bruce offers an amusing illustration of what he means:

Imagine you are born into a small stable society – the anthropologists' tribe by the lagoon – in which everyone believes that the giant squid is God. Every important life-event (births, marriages, deaths, and so on) has attached to it Squid-worshipping events. Every day, in hundreds of small bits of interaction, the divinity of the Squid is evidenced by such things as explaining bad weather by the anger of the Squid and casually dropping 'The Squid be blessed' into conversation. In such a world, the idea that the Squid is God is not a belief; it is a fact. It is just how the world is and is nearly incontestable for anyone raised in that society. Now imagine that a sudden increase in population and in the ease of travel means that the Squid tribe comes into contact with three or four other civilizations, none of which worships the Squid. Suddenly the divinity of the Squid is not a fact; it is a belief and it is a belief that is earnestly contested. The Squid tribe may still have faith in the Squid and may even start missionary societies to convert others to Squid worship, but they can never return to the earlier condition of a naïvely taken-for-granted world-view.[6]

What this illustrates for Bruce is that religious belief is no longer a matter of necessity but is instead a question of preference, and when it is a matter of preference some people will choose not to believe. This is especially the case when the choice for no belief lacks any community sanction. This leads to Bruce's second point about the breakdown of community. However, before I discuss this it is worth pointing out a problem with Bruce's example of the Squid-worshipping society. It is the sociological dilemma of the insider/observer division. Bruce's analysis that the truthfulness of the religious belief must change in a pluralist context because an alternative exists is correct for the observer. For an observer, as soon as a choice exists then the truthfulness of the original belief is relative. However, this is not the case for a believer. It is possible for the believer to have no reduction in the truthfulness of their beliefs in light of a new, alternative viewpoint appearing. This is achieved through the simple expedient, as it implied in the example, of knowing the alternative is incorrect. If the alternative is dismissed as false then the religious pluralism disappears. For a believer, truth in the face of no alternative and truth in the face of false alternatives does nothing to diminish the extent of the truthfulness.

What does change, however, is the relationship between the religious beliefs and the society in which they are dominant. This is Bruce's second point in relation to the breakdown of community. Small, tight-knit communities were able to control and monitor the beliefs and moral behaviour of their inhabitants. Effective policing was carried out by the small community for itself. Furthermore, religious beliefs permeated every aspect of the life of the community. Every important event was marked by a religious ritual, ranging from the economic, such as the celebration of harvest, to the domestic; namely births, marriages and deaths. If people failed to perform the proper ceremonies then the community would know and they would act. Religion thrives in this communal atmosphere. But, when the community breaks up under the conditions of modernization such as the move to the city or the factory, so also the dominant belief system collapses. Beliefs and practices are no longer policed by the small community. With the introduction of social fragmentation and the breakdown of community comes religious freedom and choice. Such freedom and choice meant fewer people would adhere to the practices of former generations. The breakup of community meant religious rebellion was not so noticeable and no longer led to community sanction. What has disappeared is the unquestioned status of the single overarching moral and religious system to which everyone was forced to belong. Modernization is a combination of religious pluralism and impersonal and largely anonymous social conditions, leading to the marginalization of religious practice and belief. Bruce states that the first response of the Church was to try to utilize the power of the state to enforce religious conformity. However, the social cost of seeking to use the law to combat powerful cultural change was too great, so the Church was forced to step back and allow modernization to wreak its inevitable havoc.

The third element of modernization which has damaged the Church so severely is rationalization. This is again about a changed mindset. What Bruce argues is very similar to the point I made in Chapter Two about the way in which science has replaced religion as Western society's dominant technology. However, Bruce does not only mean the clash between science and religion when he talks about rationality, nor does he mean the clash in the traditional sense. Rationality refers to the process and systems by which society makes its decisions. In rational society, routines and rules are applied to situations which are justified on grounds independent of the individual implementing the rules. So there are criteria for establishing whether any individual is entitled to free welfare benefits which are independent of the biases and prejudices of the official who administers the application. In fact, any decision would be repeated by any official who would have to follow the same criteria. This modern mentality is inimical to the religious mentality. It is concerned with procedural questions rather than with the big questions of philosophy and theology. Public discussions can be about efficiency and appropriate procedures without needing to bother with ends or meanings. So religion is pushed out of the public square.

It is only at this point that Bruce brings the subject of science into the discussion. He argues that most people do not abandon religion because they have studied Darwin, empathized with Galileo or poured over German biblical critics. When intellectual debates about the relationship between the Genesis accounts and evolution have occurred, they have been the preserve of a select few. But this does not mean science has not impacted on the Church. What has happened is that a scientific mentality has marginalized religion. This mentality is concerned with the operations of cause and effect. It seeks answers and solutions which are entirely natural, shunning the supernatural to the realm of myth. So if a plane crashes the immediate question is: What caused the crash? Was it a mechanical fault, human error or terrorist activity? The question is not: In what ways have the gods been angered? Religion enters the fray as either a comfort for those who are injured or bereaved or as a last resort when science, usually medical science, has failed. This scientific mentality is compatible with the bureaucratic mentality which makes welfare decisions on behalf of society. But neither are compatible with a religious mentality. So it is that science and bureaucracy dominate our public discussions – what is called 'rationalization' – whilst religion is a purely private matter for individual decision. The truthfulness of religion's claims cannot be subject to this type of rational investigation and so are relegated to the subjective realm.

Bruce's conclusion is that these aspects of modern society, social fragmentation, the breakdown of community and rationalization, combine to make the West mainly secular. He expresses the point well himself:

> It is not an accident that most modern societies are largely secular. Industrialization brought with it a series of social changes – the fragmentation of the life-world, the decline of community, the rise of bureaucracy, technological consciousness – which together made religion less arresting and less plausible than it had been in pre-modern societies.[7]

The notion that modernization leads to secularization is not without its critics. I shall examine the most important criticisms in the sections which follow. As we progress through the criticisms and their discussion, for Bruce is well aware of the many criticisms and has replied to them in his various books, the question which guides us is how far does this account of the rise of secularism deepen our understanding of the religious and cultural identity of Western society. The issue for the secularization thesis is that it creates a picture of societies progressively abandoning religious beliefs and practices as it grows in the secular scientific mindset. As the critics point out, the evidence is that religion has a persistence which raises serious questions about the corrosive power of modernizing society. This is the case not only in countries outside of the West but also within its boundaries.

Believing Without Belonging

The secularization thesis accounts for the decline in church affiliation and attendance in Western society. The statistics for church attendance and membership, as well as for baptisms, weddings and funerals, show that overall churchgoing is in decline compared with the Victorian period. However, alongside these statistics are another set which show that the figures for belief in God and for people identifying themselves as Christian are remarkably high. We have already seen that, in the UK government census of 2001, on average just over 70 per cent of people identified themselves as Christian. The figures for belief in God are comparable. The *European Values Study* shows that on average just over 77 per cent of Europeans reported they believed in God.[8] In some countries, notably Roman Catholic areas such as Ireland, Italy, Portugal and Spain, the figure was around the 90 per cent mark. In more liberal and historically Protestant nations the figures are lower, with Sweden being by far the lowest at 53 per cent. Sweden is the exception, with the Netherlands and France recording just over 60 per cent, and Denmark, Belgium, Germany and the UK around the 70 per cent mark. The persistence of belief in God has led some scholars to suggest that, whilst there is a clear decline in allegiance to the Church, people still maintain a religious faith. Professor Grace Davie coined the helpful phrase that people are 'believing without belonging'.[9] People believe in God but they do not attend a local church. As Davie is aware there is much local variation in religious practice and belief, and so the notion of believing without belonging is not meant as an accurate description of every circumstance. Rather, it is an alternative to the secularization thesis which takes account of the strength and resilience of belief in God in Western Europe. It is another way of reading the data and thinking about Western religious identity which does not assume inevitable decline.

The response to the idea of believing without belonging has been to question what is meant by people when they say they believe in God. The notion is undoubtedly very soft when compared with the harder indicators of religious practice such as churchgoing. Bruce argues that when people say they believe in God they mean no more than that they think of themselves as a good and decent person. Part of their personal sense of what being moral is includes belief in God. This is not the same as stating a belief in the Christian idea of God. The difficulty with Bruce's argument here is that he is not taking people at face value. At some point you have to trust what people say in response to questions or cease to bother interviewing them. This said, when more detailed questions are asked about belief in God then it is clear people are not subscribing to a form of Christian orthodoxy. Belief in a personal God or in the notion of a God that saves humanity is generally less common than a general belief in God. Bruce further believes that the figures for belief will follow the figures for church affiliation but at a slower pace. Decline in religious belief will follow the decline in religious practice. The key point that separates him and Davie is whether the two sets of statistical indicators must be related. Davie thinks they should be treated separately, Bruce that one will follow the other. The evidence is ambiguous as the figures for belief do show some signs of decline, especially when people are asked in more detail about Christian beliefs. However, the willingness of people to state a belief in God and call themselves Christian is so high compared with church attendance that something is happening which requires further explanation. The disparity between less than 8 per cent church attendance and over 70 per cent stated belief in the existence of God and self-designation as Christian is at the very least highly unusual.

The Question of Christian Identity

The secularization thesis, as proposed by Bruce, depends on two key propositions. The first is that there must be something we can identify as Christianity so that we can say it has declined. The second is that there must have been a high point of Christian practice and belief compared with which the current levels are lower. If these propositions are not proven then the situation we have now, the notion of believing without belonging, might well be a change or development in Christian faith which will not lead to greater secularism.

The idea that Christianity may be changing its identity, and, for example, no longer includes majority church attendance, is resisted by Bruce. For Bruce, Christian identity must be to a certain extent static. This is not to say that all versions of Christianity are the same; they clearly are not. However, there are core elements which must be in place. Bruce uses the analogy of the football fan to make his point:

> Only a little facetiously, I will summarize the counter-argument by using again the case of someone who asserts that he is a keen football fan but when pressed admits that he has not been to a game since his father stopped taking him at the age of 5, never watches matches on the television, does not read the football sections of newspapers, does not support any team, does not encourage his son to attend matches, and cannot name any prominent footballer.[10]

Bruce is of course correct to say that anyone who has nothing to do whatsoever with football is not a football fan. But his illustration raises the problem of identity, because it asks at what point it is legitimate to call someone a football fan. Must they have a season ticket to their local club and attend all away matches, or is it enough to be able to name one prominent player such as David Beckham? The former would exclude all but the most devoted fan, whilst the latter would seem to include almost everyone on the planet; and there are degrees between these two extremes. Is it enough to follow the results of your team in the papers but never attend matches? Are you a fan if you go to one or two games a season and regularly watch the team on television? The more these questions of degree are pursued the more prominent becomes the follow up question, namely: Who is it who decides what makes a true fan? More pertinently for this discussion: Who is it who decides what counts as being a true Christian? And who is it who decides what counts as proper belief in God or a religious rather than secular identity? Advocates of the notion of modernization assume that the definition has been set at some point in the past. But this then means the definition has been set at some point in the past and cannot change significantly in the present and future. The idea that there is one fixed definition of what Christianity was, which can act as the benchmark for present day belief and practice, is highly problematic. As I shall explore in the next chapter, this is a controversial assumption.

The question of Christian orthodoxy raises the issue of popular religion. What are we to make of an individual's claim that they are justified in the eyes of God if they do not behave in ways traditionally called Christian? At this point it is worth mentioning two studies highlighted by Hugh McLeod and, in the case of Sarah Williams, Jeremy Morris.[11] The studies, by Williams and Richard Sykes, take the secularization debate in a new direction through the study of popular religious beliefs. What they demonstrate is not only the persistence of religious belief when practice has been abandoned, but also a considered justification for the lack of church affiliation. Williams quotes a Mrs Cotton, who was born in Peckham in 1910. She said:

I always say you don't have to go to church, cos a lot of 'em when they go to this service and that what are

they?...When they say about going to church. I've seen
so much of it and the next moment they're in the
boozer and there's a few of them, I know they're hard-
working ladies, they think they're God's saints but
they're not. That's when I say as long as I'm a clean
living person who cares? ...As I say when the Lord calls
me there's nothing wrong I've done all my life. But no,
no. I've brought my children up decent and respectable
and they bring their children up the same.[12]

What is interesting here is that not only has official Church
teaching about attendance been challenged, but a rival ethical
system has been constructed with the promise of salvation
attached. It is possible to be a good person, and argue one's
point at the Day of Judgment, without going to church.
Furthermore, some of those who do go to church are open to
the charge of hypocrisy, a charge from which presumably their
churchgoing will not save them.

What the two studies illustrate is that people are able to
construct their religious belief system in a manner they would
think of as good, and possibly Christian, without needing the
sanction of the Church or in fact actually going to church. In
other words, we can presume that religious belief can survive
without concurrent church attendance and in some instances
it may actually thrive. Related to this notion of popular
religion is Grace Davie's concept of vicarious religion.[13] Davie
argues that people may not attend church, but they still want
the Church to exist and to fulfil a certain role. People have
expectations of the Church and its clergy, hence the interest
when clergy are caught by the press behaving in less than
Christian ways. There is an ownership of the Church by
people who would not count themselves as Church members or
even especially religious people. These concepts of popular
religion and vicarious religion are very important for an analysis of the religious and cultural identity of Western secular
society. This can be seen most clearly when I discuss the
medieval period. Prior to that, however, it is necessary to see

how the discussion of the Middle Ages features in the debates about the secularization thesis.

One of the criticisms levelled at the secularization thesis is that it depends on an idealized notion of Christianity in the past. For there to have been a significant enough decline in church affiliation to lead to the idea of secularization, then there must have been a period of high church attendance and support. The disputed period is the Middle Ages. The argument is that in fact churchgoing was not universal during the medieval period and that levels of belief were extremely low. This was because clergy and laity were often badly educated, churches were thinly spread out and so some distance from rural communities, and people were generally impious and irreligious. If religious belief and practice were low during the Middle Ages then what is happening now in secular society cannot be a decline from times past. It is a continuation of what is normal.

The discussion of Christian belief and practice during the Middle Ages is very important for understanding the secularism of Western society. I shall investigate how and why this is the case in Chapters Five and Six. At this stage in the discussion two things should be said. First, the argument that Christianity is in decline can be made by referring to the Victorian period. The important comparison is with the data we have from the nineteenth century. This comparison reveals the decline in Christian practice. The question then is whether the Victorian era is a continuation of the Middle Ages in terms of Christian practice and belief or whether it is itself the exceptional period. If the latter, there is still Christian decline, but it is decline from a particular historical period, the Victorian age, which may itself be exceptional. If the former, then it is absolute Christian decline, with the strong possibility that the end point is the demise of Christianity.

The second point to note goes to the heart of what Bruce means by secularization. Bruce argues that what has led to secularization is the changed mindset of Western people before and after Modernity. Prior to Modernity, people lived in feudal societies which were hierarchical, community orientated, traditional, unchanging and religious. He has in mind the medieval village. These people were Christian and the society in which they lived suited Christianity well. Christianity was the dominant supernatural worldview. There was no effective alternative. The shift to modern society was gradual. It began sometime around the Reformation and at this stage was illustrated by the rise of individualism. As discussed, other social changes created a climate which excluded and marginalized Christian practice and belief. These are tied up with industrialization and urbanization. The exact chronology intended by Bruce is difficult to follow. The consequence was the end of religious belief. At this point Bruce is quite specific. He argues that, whatever might be said about church attendance and Christian belief during the Middle Ages, what is certain is that what predominated then was a supernatural worldview. The whole of medieval life and society was built on supernatural assumptions. Secularization is then the shift in mindset to the rational mentality of modern society. The problem with the argument is the persistent belief in God. It is possible to agree with Bruce that a shift in Western mentality has occurred at some point between the Middle Ages and now. However, that shift has not eradicated belief in God which, however it is intended or meant and whether it is identifiably Christian or not, is a belief in some form of the supernatural. In other words, there appear to be two mindsets at work in Western secular society. One is the rational mindset that Bruce identifies and that was discussed in Chapter Two. The second is an ongoing supernatural mindset which Bruce wants to deny but which repeatedly appears in the statistical evidence. It is this dual identity which requires further investigation and explanation.

The Problem of the United States of America

Western Europe has been described as the 'exceptional case' when it comes to religious belief and practice.[14] This is

because religions, especially Christianity and Islam, are important social and cultural forces in countries throughout Latin
America, Africa and Asia. What is interesting for our discussion is that the Christian religion is also a very important
phenomenon in the USA. The dilemma this raises is that,
according to all the factors identified by Bruce, the USA is a
modern country. If the secularization thesis is correct then the
USA should be exhibiting the same indications of Church
decline, as are apparent in the UK and most parts of Western
Europe. However, this is not the case; there are around about
90 per cent of North Americans who report that they believe
in God.[15] Large numbers further assent to orthodox Christian
doctrines about the nature of God and God's relationship with
humanity. About 40 per cent of Americans report that they
attend church once a week and even higher numbers once a
month. This is comparable with the peak during the Victorian
era identified by Mann in his 1851 census. In addition to these
high levels of belief and practice, Christianity also has a
high profile in US political and cultural life. We have already
identified the fears of secularists that the Republican government is dominated by right-wing Christians, notably of course
George W. Bush, and that candidates for election need to
demonstrate their Christian credentials. If there is a secular
mindset at work in Western society then it would appear to
have passed the USA by.

How are these high levels of Christian belief and practice to
be explained? One strategy is to question the figures themselves. There is some legitimacy in this approach. Churches in
the USA do not report the high levels of attendance which
should be apparent if we believe those answering opinion polls.
People are claiming to go to church when in fact they are stay-
ing at home. This in itself is an interesting phenomenon.
There is something in North American cultural identity which
regards churchgoing as desirable. Furthermore, it calls into
question the extent to which Americans are going to church.
This said, the discrepancy in the figures does not mean church
affiliation levels are as low as in Western Europe. The process

of secularization is clearly slower in the USA than in other parts of the West.

Bruce explains the surprising resilience of Christian belief and practice in the USA utilizing two important social concepts. These are the notions of cultural defence and cultural transition.[16] These concepts are tied closely to ethnicity. Bruce argues that religious identity acquires a new and heightened significance when an ethnic group feels itself to be under threat. This is the case if the religious identity follows the contours of the ethnic identity. This it frequently does. So, for example, the Orthodox faith of Serbians and the Roman Catholicism of Croats became very important during the violent conflicts following the break up of Yugoslavia. Likewise, Protestantism and Catholicism are very important in Northern Ireland because of the social and political divisions between communities. The idea of cultural transition equally emphasizes the close connection between ethnicity and religious faith. What Bruce argues is that religious identity can become important for an ethnic group if members of that group move to a new environment. This applies usually in the case of immigration. Religious faith is a valuable cultural support for those needing security in a new and sometimes hostile location.

The applicability of these two concepts to the USA is clear. In many ways the USA is an immigrant country with new ethnic communities settling and developing all the time. This has two effects. The earlier immigrant groups feel themselves under threat from new communities and seek to reassert their religious and cultural identity as a form of defence. The newer immigrant groups use their religious and cultural identity to ease into the new country and establish themselves. It might only be after they feel established, and no longer threatened by either the move itself or the earlier immigrant groups, that they begin to relinquish their religious loyalty and display signs of secularization.

There are two important points to be drawn from Bruce's analysis. The first is that what he describes would have occurred during the early period of urbanization in the UK. It would have been to a lesser extent, but people and communities shifting to the cities in search of new forms of employment still would have experienced the dislocation of immigrant groups. In which case we would expect to see high levels of religious belief and practice at the beginning of the modernization period. The second point is that as a cultural force modernization is not especially strong. The changed mindset has a fragility which means it can be abandoned, or at the very least put on hold, during times of crisis. Bruce's analysis seems to suggest a flexibility in the modernized mindset so that, when necessary, it can be put to one side so that more basic requirements of security are met.

The problem of US Christianity leads us to one of three possible conclusions. It may be that the secularization thesis proposed by Bruce simply is not the explanation for the decline in church affiliation. If a highly modernized country is not becoming more secular then a new explanation for the situation in Western Europe is required. Or the opposite is the case, and it may be that Bruce is correct and this will become evident in time. As communities settle down, and as the country grows older, so the need for religion as a tool for cultural defence or transition diminishes. Once this occurs the normal patterns of secularization will emerge. Or it may be that we do not need to choose between modern and pre-modern mindsets. It may well be that the two mindsets can coexist side by side. What happens then is that local social and cultural factors may well bring one mindset more to the fore than another. This is the case in the USA today with its high-profile religious agenda. In other countries and at different points in history a more secular, modernist mindset may well come to the fore. An example here would be the strong anti-clericalism and secularism of France, reacting against the conservatism of the ancien regime. Likewise, the important role played by Roman Catholicism in Poland during the final period of Soviet Communist rule. There are many other examples that might also be given. The important point at this stage is not to accept the dichotomy between either secularism or religious faith, implied in the notion of a changed mindset resulting from new and different social conditions. The two mindsets may well exist side by side.

The Collapse of Christianity During the 1960s

The final challenge to Bruce's account of secularization is the most recent and most substantial.[17] In some ways it tells a very similar story to Bruce. Dramatic social change led to a severe downturn in the fortunes of the Church and Christianity; however, there are important differences. This time the key period is the 1960s, specifically 1963, when changing social patterns, increased liberalism and a revolutionary new identity for women led to a dramatic and rapid fall in church attendance and support. What is interesting is that although statistics are fundamental to the argument they do not dominate the discussion. Rather, Callum Brown wants to describe the bigger sociological picture and for this he needs to employ oral testimonies and a detailed examination of popular literature. However, despite the claim to a post-modern methodology the analysis begins with statistics.

Although he would not intend this, Steve Bruce's description of secularization creates an impression of a linear, progressive decline in the fortunes of the Church. The high point is 1851 and the low point is now. In fact, the decline was not so straightforward. Different indicators of religious practice show signs of both decline and growth. The numbers for Church membership illustrate what is better thought of as wave-like patterns of decline and fall. The number of Church members grew from the 1840s to a peak in 1904–5. The growth was rapid until 1863, and then slowed down or fluctuated between decline and growth until the early twentieth century. Between the beginning of the century and 1950, there was a decline in Church membership; however, this was gradual and modest. The figures for church attendance show a modest decline for the period between the later half of the nineteenth century and the 1940s. Brown speculates that this decline may in fact be the result in fewer people attending church twice on a Sunday and so should not be seen as a decrease in the total number of people attending church, or at most a very small decrease.[18] During the first half of the twentieth century, the number of marriages performed in church, in contrast to a registry office, declined only very slightly, whilst the number of baptisms actually increased, as did overall enrolment in Sunday School.

The major exception to the picture of decline was the post-war period. Brown argues that the 1940s and 1950s 'witnessed the greatest church growth that Britain had experienced since the mid-nineteenth century'.[19] He writes that:

> During the late 1940s and first half of the 1950s, organized Christianity experienced the greatest per annum growth in church membership, Sunday school enrollment, Anglican confirmations and presbyterian recruitment of its baptised constituency since the eighteenth century.[20]

The new religious mood was illustrated by the popularity of mass revival meetings. In particular, the Billy Graham crusades demonstrated the new culture of Christianity. These were supported by levels of visiting and tract distribution not seen since the Victorian period. What was the reason for this increased Church popularity? Brown argues that the immediate post-war period was a time of traditionalism and austerity. The austerity was a result of the economic cost of the war. The traditionalism came from the desire to return to the pre-war social status quo. Family values, notions of the importance of home and of piety, especially for women, were back on the agenda. This was in all likelihood a reaction to the end of the war and the returning soldiers. Whilst they had been away women had left the home and worked in factories and offices in place of the fighting men. Now women were publicly urged back into the home to make way for the men and to reward them for their courage and suffering.

The reason Brown offers this analysis becomes clear when we look at the next stage of the story. It was during and after the 1960s that Christian belief and practice collapsed. The collapse has been dramatic and, Brown would argue, fatal. In all religious indicators, the numbers of those who associated with the Christian Church has plummeted to historically low levels. The reason for this collapse is twofold. In part it is a result of social change. The 1960s saw an end of the traditional values that had dominated the late 1940s and 1950s and the emergence of a society characterized by liberalism. The totem of this shift in British culture was the trial over Lawrence's novel *Lady Chatterley's Lover*. Perhaps more significant events were the legalization of abortion and homosexuality in 1967, changes to make divorce easier in 1969, and the development of a radical youth culture and student agitation in the late 1960s and early 1970s. The Christian Church suffered enormously from this breakdown of traditional society.

Even more significant, however, was the emergence of the women's movement. Brown had argued that a key factor in the high levels of Victorian Church allegiance was the predominant cultural notion of a pious woman. The dominant identity presented to women in literature and society was of a good woman. This good woman was moral, disciplined and religious; furthermore, she had an important social role. It was the good wife who could reform a wayward husband or son. The loving, responsible and pious daughter could rescue a drunkard father, a gambling brother or an immoral fiancé. Women were consistently told that if they wished to be true to their gender then they should be good and pious and that meant at the very least church attendance.

In the 1960s this changed. Second-wave feminism reshaped the image of what a typical woman should be like. Brown analyses women's magazines to demonstrate the shift. During the 1940s and 1950s magazines presumed the woman would be in the home caring for the man of the house and for children.

In the 1960s new publications emerged which discussed women's careers, looked at fashion, assumed an interest in entertainment and spoke frankly about women's sexual issues. Women, the magazines assumed, were no longer restricted to the home and were no longer exclusively pious. And the new magazines were popular. Magazines such as *Housewife* were replaced by *She* and *Cosmopolitan*, which dared to have women discussing social issues as well as careers and sexuality.

The consequences of this shift in femininity for the Church was disastrous. It was women who had come to church in large numbers and it was women who had been the bedrock of support for baptisms, weddings and Sunday schools. For them to stop supporting the Church was an enormous blow. Added to this it was women who had often pressurized their men to come to church. If the women themselves were no longer attending then their menfolk were unlikely to come on their own. This double blow to the Church resulted in what Brown has identified as the collapse in Church support and Christian culture since the 1960s. The Church was unable to adapt to and attract the new woman of the second half of the twentieth century and so it rapidly declined.

Callum Brown's analysis of church decline is a major challenge to Bruce's ideas about secularization and modernization. There is no room in Bruce's theory for the impressive resurgence of Christianity in the middle of the twentieth century. Under the conditions of modernized society, Christianity should not be able to grow. Nor did Bruce pick up on the dramatic fall in church allegiance during and after the 1960s, and the role in this fall played by women. This said, Brown arrives at a very similar place to Bruce. Both reach the end of the twentieth century with a thesis which explains church decline. Both are left with the resilience of belief in God and the desire of a large majority of the population to call themselves Christian. Furthermore, nothing which Brown argues removes the value of Bruce's analysis of a rational mindset, which in some ways marginalizes religious belief. In fact, what Brown illustrates is what I concluded above; namely, this rational mindset is very soft and liable to be shelved when social or cultural factors come to the fore. This might be ethnic insecurity, such as immigration into the USA, or it might be the reinvention of identity, such as experienced by women during the 1940s and 1950s.

Conclusion

The range of the discussion in this chapter means it is helpful to have a set of concluding remarks which sum up the point we have reached in our study so far. To begin with it is clear that the contribution of Steve Bruce to the discussion of secularization has been enormous. This does not mean, however, that we have to agree with his analysis. In fact, we are left with some important questions. First, if Bruce is correct about the changed rational mindset, and as a result of the discussion in the Chapter One we are inclined to suppose he is, then when did this change occur and how? To address this question we need to look at the period known as the Enlightenment.

Second, Bruce argues that the medieval period was a time of supernatural belief and this contrasts with Western society. We have argued that supernatural beliefs, especially the belief in God, can coexist with the rational mentality identified by Bruce. The question is what might this coexistence look like. We have begun to explore this question with our descriptions of popular and vicarious religion. These ideas themselves provoked questions about the nature of Christian identity. To what extent is Christian identity static? I address this question in the next chapter. I then go on to suggest that a study of medieval religious belief and behaviour will develop our understanding of Western secular society, in particular in relation to the notions of popular and vicarious religion.

The work of Callum Brown is a substantial challenge to Bruce's analysis. Although we end up with a similar picture of church decline, the route by which this is reached is very different. Brown has a weight of statistical and cultural evidence to support his analysis that the 1960s were a crucial period for understanding the demise of church affiliation and attendance. What is also clear from Brown's work is that the Victorian period was itself a time of exceptional religious activity. Compared with this period, most eras would seem to show a pattern of church decline. I have not investigated this aspect of Brown's study in any detail in this chapter and so I explore this further in Chapter Eight. Before that, however, we shall explore the question of Christian identity.

Chapter Four

The Reinvention of
Christianity by Ordinary
People

It is clear from the evidence that there has been a decline in church attendance and affiliation. It is also clear that people in very large numbers are still describing themselves as Christian and stating that they believe in God. One conclusion we can draw from these facts is that Christianity is changing. It is not the only conclusion that could be drawn as we saw in Chapter Three. However, it is certainly possible that what might well be happening is that ordinary people are reinventing Christianity. They are constructing a version of Christianity that does not include regular church attendance or orthodox doctrinal beliefs. This reinvention implies that Christianity has a fluid, unstable identity.

In this chapter, I will investigate this notion of reinvention. I shall argue that the history of Christianity has always been one of transition and reinvention. What we are describing as a twenty-first century phenomenon is a normal part of the life of the Church. Historically, Christianity has spread by being formed and reformed in different cultures. The focus of the study will be on the Early Church. This is to demonstrate how reinvention has been a part of the life of Christianity from the very beginning. I shall then discuss some of the problems that arise if we have such a fluid notion of Christian identity and some of the challenges to this argument. It will include an examination of whether the person of the historical Jesus provides a stable platform on which to construct Christian identity. It will also include a discussion of how Christianity can be a critical witness in society if its identity is shaped by society. The chapter will conclude with a discussion of what it might mean to describe a set of ideas or values as Christian if this has no stable, identifiable meaning.

The Spread of Christianity

Christianity has always been a missionary religion. From its very earliest days it has crossed national and cultural borders. To understand the process of reinvention we need to turn to mission history. There are two concepts which will further our analysis. The first is the idea of paradigm shifts. This is taken from the philosophy of science and in particular a book by Thomas Kuhn, called *The Structure of Scientific Revolutions*. The second is the notion of 'ongoing inculturation', which is a term employed by the Dutch missiologist Anton Wessels.[1]

The outstanding writer on missiology at the end of the twentieth century was David Bosch. His major work, *Transforming Mission*, explores mission history through the concept of paradigm shifts. A paradigm is a means of dividing up history into distinctive periods. Thomas Kuhn had argued that the history of science could be analysed by recognizing that in different historical periods there were dominant sets of assumptions which guided scientific thought. These assumptions characterized the paradigm and controlled what was valid or true at that time. Paradigms changed when the assumptions of the old paradigm ceased to be able to explain the majority of what was being observed. The old paradigm broke down when there were too many exceptions to its basic rules and so it was unable to provide adequate explanations. At that point a new paradigm had to take over. This had a different set of assumptions which directed scientific thought until it too was unable to explain the majority of phenomena being observed. Kuhn believed that his analysis of paradigms was of limited applicability and only appropriate for the study of the natural sciences. He specifically forbade its use outside of scientific history. However, this did not prevent other scholars recognizing the value of the notion of paradigm shifts to divide up the history of their own discipline. They therefore disregarded his injunction.

Professor Hans Küng employed the concept of paradigms and paradigm shifts to divide up the history of Christianity. He followed Kuhn closely in his description of what was meant by a paradigm. It was 'an entire constellation of beliefs, values, techniques, and so on shared by members or a given community'.[2] In other words, it is an entire way of thinking about a topic. It involves both the subject being considered and also the way in which that subject is interpreted. When a paradigm changes then all that is meant by the topic changes as well. In this sense a paradigm shift is comprehensive and all-encompassing. It is also rare.

David Bosch was attracted by the idea of understanding Christianity's history as a succession of paradigm shifts and so employed Küng's method for his study of mission history. Bosch analyses six different paradigms. These are: the apocalyptic paradigm of primitive Christianity; the Hellenistic paradigm of the patristic period; the medieval Roman Catholic paradigm; the Protestant (Reformation) paradigm; the modern Enlightenment paradigm; and the emerging ecumenical paradigm.[3] It is not necessary to discuss each of these paradigms in detail. If what we are saying about the fluid identity of Christianity is correct then we would expect to see a paradigm shift in the earliest history of the Church. This we do when Christianity moves out of its Jewish context to the Hellenistic culture of the Roman Empire.

The first paradigm shift was from the Jewish context of Jesus and the first apostles to the Greco-Roman world of the Early Church. This Bosch describes as the shift from the apocalyptic theology of the biblical era to the Hellenistic Church of the patristic period.[4] The shift was fundamental. It can almost be equated with creation of a new religion. It was the first move that Christianity made and the consequences of the shift were enormous. Bosch quotes from Paul Knitter to describe the essential change that occurred:

> It was a transformation not only in the liturgical, sacramental life of the church and in the structures of its organization and legislation, but also in its *doctrine* – that is, in the *understanding* of the revelation that had given birth to it. The early Christians did not simply express in Greek thought what they already knew; rather, they discovered, through Greek religious and philosophical insights, what had been revealed to them. The doctrines of the trinity and of the divinity of Christ...for example, would not be what they are today if the church had not reassessed itself and its doctrines in the light of the new historical, cultural situations during the third through the sixth centuries.[5]

The Christian religion ceased to be entirely apocalyptic and dominated by a concern about the end of history. It gave up hoping for the imminent return of the Messiah and the inauguration of the final reign of God. Instead, it became an expression of Hellenistic philosophy. Its efforts focused on describing the attributes of God. It sought to understand the relationship between God and humanity in philosophical terms through the person of Christ. This was a fundamental shift in identity, not merely its organization, nor only in rituals and practices, but also the actual content of what was believed. It was because of the encounter with Greek philosophy that what became orthodox Christian doctrine could actually be discovered. It raises the controversial question of whether the historical figure, Jesus of Nazareth, would have had the cultural or intellectual tools necessary to comprehend Christianity's later manifestation.

In what specific ways did the new Hellenistic Christianity differ from its Jewish precursor? The impact was felt in both ethics and doctrine. The earliest Christian writers, beginning with Paul, appropriated material from Greco-Roman moral philosophers.[6] In doctrine, the Early Church shaped faith and theology by employing the tools of Greek philosophy. Christianity became a religion capable of reflecting on essential being and nature, and less concerned with action and history. Bosch argues: 'The God of the Old Testament and primitive Christianity came to be identified with the general idea of the God of Greek metaphysics; God is referred to as Supreme Being, substance, principle, unmoved mover. Ontology (God's being) became more important than history (God's deeds).' As Christianity shifted into Hellenistic culture, so doctrine became more important than ethics. A comparison of the Sermon on the Mount and the Nicene Creed demonstrate the point. Bosch wrote: 'The former outlines a mode of conduct without any specific appeal to a set of precepts. The entire tenor of the Sermon is ethical; it is devoid of metaphysical speculation. The latter, in contrast, is structured within a metaphysical framework, makes a number of doctrinal state-ments, and says nothing about the believer's conduct.'

Bosch argues that the shift was a positive development. The change in identity provided the fledgling Church with the intellectual, especially philosophical, tools necessary to develop from being a minority Jewish sect to a worldwide religion, albeit tied to the fortunes of Western political empires.[7] It was Greek philosophy that equipped the Church to produce 'a fundamentally rational account of how human beings attain appropriate knowledge of God, and to do all this with a combination of intellectual rigor and a deep faith com-mitment'. This is true. But the question it creates is what is left of substance of the Jewish-formed Christianity of Jesus of Nazareth which provides the religion with its stable identity. Is there something identifiably Christian which has a coherent historical relationship with Jesus of Nazareth? Or did Christianity become something new?

Bosch's initial answer to these questions seems to suggest Christianity is by its nature repeatedly changeable. Christianity had a revolutionary character. Bosch argues that Christians should not be worried that during the period of the paradigm shift the identity of Christianity changed so dramatically. The reason for this is that Christianity is at heart a religion of the Incarnation. One of its core doctrines is that God became a human being. The Divine immersed Godself in an alternative context. In history, the uncreated God became a fully created human. Likewise, the Church will enter into new contexts and cultures. It does this not as a foreign body hygienically separated from local culture, but as a fully integrated member of society.[8] At this point it seems that an entirely fluid Christian identity is possible for Bosch.

However, as Bosch explores the sweep of the first few centuries of Christianity, his position becomes more conservative. Bosch argues that the triumph of what we now call orthodoxy was possible because of the limits entailed by the doctrine of the Incarnation. In its conflicts with heretical ideas, Catholic Christianity held an advantage because it adopted both Hellenistic thought forms and a substantial memory of its Jewish beginnings. The Church could resist those heretics who wanted to make Christianity more Jewish, the Ebionites and Montanists, and those who wanted it to be more Hellenistic, such as the Gnostics. When the Church was confronted by the threat of heretical groups, it responded by holding on to what Bosch called 'the most fundamental and inalienable elements of the Christian faith: the canonicity of the Old Testament, the historicity of the humanity of Jesus, the bodily resurrection of Jesus from the dead'.[9] In other words, although Christianity was transformed by its relocation as a Hellenistic theology, it clung to some core elements which protected its integrity and identity. Despite being offered the temptation of an absolutely new identity, it remained true to its essence. The Christianity of the Hellenistic Early Church might be a new religion, but it was one which was still in discernible continuity with the Jewish beginnings of Jesus of Nazareth. This continuity was more than nominal; it played a part in shaping the new religion.

In this analysis, Bosch follows the work of Hans Küng. It is through continuity and discontinuity that paradigm shifts work in history. Küng argues that to understand the way in which theology develops, then 'we have to avoid the choice not only between an absolutist and a relativist view, but between a radical continuity and a radical discontinuity'. He goes on: 'Every paradigm change shows at the same time continuity and discontinuity, rationality and irrationality, conceptual stability and conceptual change, evolutionary and revolutionary elements.'[10] What this means is that the religious and cultural differences between alternate paradigms are significant but not absolute. From the evidence of early Christian mission it is easy to discern the radical discontinuity. A new religion has been shaped which is some distance from the Jewish identity of Jesus of Nazareth and the first apostles. As is clear from the records in the Acts of the Apostles, many non-Jews were not prepared to become culturally Jewish. The development of doctrine further shows how far Christianity travelled from its Jewish roots. But Bosch and Küng argue that there must also be some continuity. For Bosch, the figure of the historical Jesus is an important continuity. More controversially so is the bodily resurrection of Christ. At this point the history Bosch tells begins to resemble the best of all worlds. Christianity in its present form is also Christianity in its best form, and this is because of its ideal history. Bosch provides an historical account of the spread of Christianity which ends up being a eulogy to the efforts of early Christians to change when change was desirable, and remain unchanging when heresies threatened. Such a history seems unlikely. It takes a series of historical incidents and turns them into this ideal account. Bosch is helpful in showing why Christianity would change radically by demonstrating the impact of new cultures and societies. In the end, however, his conservatism leads to a rather idealistic picture of Christian mission history. At this point the work of Anton Wessels is helpful in offering a fuller picture of what happens to Christianity as it shifts paradigms.

The Ongoing Inculturation of Christianity

Anton Wessels, former Professor of Missiology and Religion in
the Free University of Amsterdam, wrote his book *Europe: Was
it Ever Really Christian?* in order to investigate how Christianity
first entered into European culture. A culture becomes
Christian when it accepts baptism and other rituals, including
attendance at Mass on certain days.[11] Under this definition,
much of England, France and Germany had adopted Christianity by 750 CE. Wessels investigated how it was that Christianity
spread. His central idea was the notion of 'ongoing inculturation'. This described the way in which the new religion,
Christianity, integrated with the already existing indigenous
faith and culture. Wessels was suspicious of the depth with
which Christianity was received. He argued that even up until
the Reformation the Christian religion was a 'thin veneer'
in Northern Europe. He was even unsure of whether it was
possible to talk reasonably of medieval Christianity.[12] The
question for us is what is it about the early spread of
Christianity that leads Wessels to these conclusions?

Wessels identified two processes by which Christianity
spread. These come from Richard H. Niebuhr's analysis of the
relationship between Christianity and culture. They are
Christ the abolisher of culture and Christ the transformer of
culture.[13] The first, Christ, the abolisher of culture, is
intended to describe the way in which Christianity can enter
a culture and sweep away all previous belief systems.
Christianity replaces the vanquished culture with a new set of
beliefs, rituals and practices. To illustrate the point, Wessels
described how in 724 Boniface cut down an old oak tree dedicated to Donar. Boniface wanted to demonstrate the errors of
the indigenous pre-Christian belief systems, something he
achieved when 'the giant oak fell to the ground and Boniface
remained unharmed'. As a result, 'the pagans recognised the
superior power of the Christian God and came in hordes to be
baptized'.[14] Another illustration of the same process is taken
from the life of Martin of Tours (*c.* 316 to *c.* 397 CE). Martin

journeyed through Burgundy destroying temples, smashing up idols and cutting down holy trees. Gregory of Tours (*c.* 539 to *c.* 595), in his *History of the Franks*, described how his predecessor Martin visited the pagan temples 'like a real iconoclast'. This is one method of Christian growth.

However, this pattern of Christ as the abolisher of culture is not Wessels' main concern. He is more interested in the alternate model of Christ as the transformer of culture. This is the style of Christian mission which Wessels believed was more prevalent and successful. In this methodology Christianity takes over the previous indigenous religion and changes it into Christianity. The indigenous faith is adopted and then transformed. An early example of this process is Pope Gregory the Great's missionary instructions to the abbot Augustine in England. A letter from Pope Gregory is preserved in the Venerable Bede's history:

> When, therefore, Almighty God shall bring you to the most revered Bishop Augustine, our brother, tell him what I have, upon mature deliberation on the affairs of the English, determined upon, viz., that the temples of the idols in that nation ought not to be destroyed; but let the idols that are in them be destroyed; let holy water be made and sprinkled in said temples, let altars be erected, and relics placed. For if those temples are well built, it is requisite that they be converted from the worship of devils to the service of the true God; that the nation, seeing that their temples are not destroyed, may remove error from their heart, and, knowing and adoring the true God, may the more familiarly resort to the places to which they have been accustomed.[15]

Pope Gregory gave permission for the places of pre-Christian religion to be transformed into Christian churches. In doing so he sets in motion a dual process of innovation and familiarity. What is new is the end of the worship of idols and the imposition of the Christian God. What remains the same is, at the very least, the geographical location of religious ritual. The question arises whether the maintenance of location and architecture ensures a continuity of religious belief. How new is the religion when the place of worship is so well known? A new language and practice is presented to the population, but the tools they possess for making sense of the new will be built on a framework of the old. This is something they are reminded of each time they journey to their familiar places of worship.

Wessels called this process of adoption and transformation 'ongoing inculturation'. The question is, when Christians adopt and transform a prior religious culture, what impact does this have on their faith? Is the Christianity also changed by the encounter? Wessels pursued these questions by examining three periods of the historical spread of Christianity: the Greco-Roman context; the Celtic contextualization; and the Germanic world. I will focus on three illustrations of the merging of pre-Christian and Christian beliefs in the spread of Christianity in the Hellenistic world.

The first area to investigate is the relationship between what was believed about the person of Jesus Christ and the pre-Christian understanding of Orpheus. What we see is a remarkable continuity between Christian and pre-Christian beliefs. Wessels argued that the 'church in the Greco-Roman world had no problem over connecting Orpheus with Christ'. Orpheus was portrayed in Greek mythology as a singer and poet who was able to charm human beings, animals and even inanimate nature with his songs. Orpheus was almost able to save his dead wife Eurydice from Hades. Unfortunately, Orpheus looked back on the journey out of Hades and Eurydice was lost forever. Wessels argued that Christians adopted the motif of the saviour singer to describe Christ. Clement of Alexandria talks about Christ 'by analogy with Orpheus as his singer', although it is Christ who is the better.[16] Eusebius of Caesarea spoke of 'Orpheus charming wild animals as Christ charmed stubborn sinners'. Wessels went on, saying certain 'apologists on the one hand had a tendency to depict Orpheus as a "teacher of the pagans", and in other circles he was portrayed as a "pre-Christian sage" who was endowed with Logos and had already proclaimed "an only God and his Christ"'. However, more significant than these occasional comparisons is what Wessels describes as the adoption of Orphic beliefs by Christians. Of particular interest is the adoption of the familiar motif of the good shepherd.

One of the ways in which people in the Hellenistic world made sense of Christ was to think of him in terms of what they already knew about Orpheus. So we find that in the catacombs the person of Jesus Christ is shown to be a shepherd, a teacher and as the singer Orpheus. It is also the case that in early Christian art Orpheus is understood to be a prefigurement of Christ and was seen at an early stage as the symbol of Christ as 'Saviour'. This type of shepherd precedes the notion of the 'good shepherd'.[17] The good shepherd was the image for Christ in early Christian literature, liturgy and art. The motif had two meanings. First, the good shepherd was a vehicle for salvation; it is he who delivers sheep safe after the journey of death. Second, there is the more idyllic notion of the pastoral figure who cares for his flock: 'The way in which "the good shepherd", "youthful and without a beard, and with a lamb on his shoulders" is depicted goes back to pre-Christian sarcophagus art, which thus becomes the vehicle of a biblical content'. Wessels argues that it was 'Greek mythology which created the decorative elements for the tombs of the first martyrs'.[18] Not only is the motif of the good shepherd important here. Orpheus' name is derived from the term for a fish and on 'a beaker from the third or fourth century before Christ Orpheus is depicted as a "fisher of men"'. In language that is recognizable from the Gospel accounts, Orpheus 'is called the fisher who fishes men living like fish in water, turned towards the light'. Wessels concludes that the motif of the fisher of men is an old motif which precedes Christianity. It was adopted by Christians and given a Christian theological meaning. The question then is to what extent was Christianity transformed by the adoption of what was believed about Orpheus.

Orpheus is but one of many examples Wessels lists of pre-Christian ideas and beliefs informing the presentation of Christianity to the Hellenist world. It is not relevant to list them all here, they are detailed in Wessels' book; however, we can examine two further important set of beliefs. These concern the Indo-Iranian god Mithras and the Saxon goddess Ostara.

In Iran the god Mithras progressed up the divine hierarchy, starting as god of treatises and then becoming god of the 'dawn', then sun god, god of life, and finally 'the victorious god of war'.[19] Mithras, as the god of war, achieved popularity amongst Roman soldiers and so devotion to the god spread throughout the Roman Empire. The emperor Aurelian introduced the festival of the god in Rome between 270 and 275 CE. Mithras, now Sol Invictus, the unconquered sun, became the god of the court and empire, replacing Jupiter. The date for the festival of Sol Invictus was 25 December, the date of the winter solstice in the Julian calendar and regarded as the paramount date for the sun.[20]

Immediately the relationship between Christ and Sol Invictus becomes clear. Wessels suggested that the celebration of the birth of Christ on this date originates in the Church of Rome from *c.* 336 CE. He goes on to argue that 'at a very early date Christ is likened to the sun, especially the *rising* sun'. In Gospel accounts of the hymn of Zechariah, Jesus is described as the 'light that shines in the darkness'. Christ was proclaimed as 'the new light', the 'true' and 'only' sun. 'Christ was also a rising "sun of righteousness"', the slogan used to convert adherents to Sol Invictus. As is well known there is a depiction of Sol Invictus on the Christian emperor Constantine's arch. As Wessels states, what seems to have happened is that the pre-Christian beliefs and values brought a new dimension to the Church's understanding of Jesus Christ. At the very least there is nothing in the biblical texts to indicate that Jesus of Nazareth was born on 25 December. Furthermore, the Christian holy day was not the Sabbath but *dies solis*, Sunday. Wessels reports that Christ is referred to as

'"Sol", "the true, spiritual sun", the "sun of the resurrection", the "sun of righteousness", the Saviour expected "as the light that comes from above"'.[21]

In the mausoleum below St Peter's in Rome, Christ Helios is represented rising from Hades to his Father. Wessels further argued that Mithras was the object of secret worship and that a part of the worship of antiquity were sacramental meals for a god who offered himself for the sake of the world. Wessels goes on to try and make links between the Eucharist, baptism and the mystery cults of the Hellenistic world, although the evidence of these connections is not especially strong.

The process through which Christianity spread by adopting local pre-Christian religions and transforming them into Christian beliefs and rituals continued after the initial movement of Christianity into the Hellenistic world. Wessels examines the spread of Christianity throughout the Celtic and Germanic worlds in the first few centuries of the Christian era. It is not necessary to repeat all Wessels' arguments and data here. It is possible to examine one important historical and theological example which can illustrate the questions and issues raised by Wessels' work.

Wessels noted that in German and English the word for Easter has no connection with the Greek *pascha*, unlike the French and Dutch. The explanation for this is that the name of Easter probably stems from the name of the Saxon goddess Eastre or Ostara, 'the goddess of eggs and spring'.[22] Wessels writes that:

> The Venerable Bede reports that in English April is called 'Eoster month'. Ostara was regarded as the goddess of the resurrection of nature after the long death of winter. The feast dedicated to her now became the Christian Easter. Eggs were eaten at the festival, and Christians preserved this custom. The egg became the symbol of the resurrection of Christ. Taking round Easter eggs and kindling Easter fire, along with the custom of a hunt for eggs, derive from the festival of

> this goddess. Possibly this custom goes back to burying
> eggs in the fields for fertility.[23]

Wessels goes on to argue that the festival of Ostara was so popular that there was no will to remove or demonize it. Instead, the early Christians simply took over the rituals and re-described them in the new discourse of Christianity. The question is what happened to Christianity in this process. How much was it re-described by the process of adoption? At one level the new Christian beliefs gave a new meaning to the old religion of the goddess. However, at the same time the preserved beliefs of the goddess, protected by the retention of the rituals associated with her worship, would have impacted on what people understood was meant by Christianity. Christianity became a festival of new life and fertility through its contact with Ostara. This is both similar to and significantly different from the associations of 'paschal'; that is, new life through sacrifice. One can imagine a twofold process at work. People could accept the new 'god' Jesus Christ as a replacement for Ostara if the Christ performed a familiar function well, and it was expedient for political, social or religious reasons. If Jesus Christ will ensure the crops grow when eggs are exchanged or planted, and if worship of Ostara is now illegal, then there is little sense in persevering with the old religion. Alongside this pragmatism one can imagine how the adoption of the rituals associated with Ostara aided the spread of the new Christian religion. As people sought to make sense of Christianity, and the new understanding of God and God's relationship with humanity, then the old beliefs and practices were an instrument of comprehension. For some, one can imagine the key to conversion was the greater power or success of the new Christ over the old goddess. But the new god Christ did the same deeds as Ostara and was understood in the same way. In these cases little that is fundamental or core has changed, only the exterior clothing of the beliefs. What is more, for a majority the continuity of beliefs is vital. It was the way sense and meaning could be made of the new religion of Christianity.

How are we to evaluate Wessels' work? The first thing to note is the implications of what is being said. Wessels argues that the process by which Christianity spread means that Christianity has no static, essential identity. Christianity was not always able to eradicate indigenous beliefs. When and where pre-Christian beliefs were popular and stubborn, then these beliefs were absorbed by Christianity. Furthermore, these pre-Christian beliefs changed what was understood to be the Christian faith. Where people had to make sense of Christian beliefs, they utilized familiar religious ideas to give meaning to the new religion. Christianity is a fluid religion and its success in spreading throughout the West may, in part, be attributed to its capacity to change and adapt. It is also important to note that this is a popular process. What we are describing here is how ordinary people converted to Christianity. They were required to make sense of the new beliefs, rituals and practices. They did this themselves, employing the religious language they knew well. It was not meant to be an intellectual, theological or philosophical exercise leading to new scholarship; it was a pragmatic adoption and transformation of Christianity, or, to use the term we employed earlier, the reinvention of Christianity as it spread into new cultures.

This raises a contemporary question: What are the limits on the fluidity of Christian identity? Can anything which has claimed to be Christian actually be so? Wessels considers this question briefly at the end of his book. He answers 'no' because of the recent experience of the rise of German Christians. Their propagation of a racist, nationalist religious ideology means he does not believe they were Christians. There is an ethical limit to the boundaries of what can be acceptable to Christians. The ongoing xenophobia in Europe, illustrated by the break up of Yugoslavia, reiterates the dangers of too easy an acceptance of limitless Christian identity. Wessels writes that 'the legitimate defence of and rise of one's own cultural identity must not in any case become un-ecumenical in a Christian perspective, a threat against the social well-being of the whole ecumene, the "inhabited world".[24] It might well be argued, however, that all this illustrates is the adoption by Wessels of liberal ethical values into his Christianity. There are no foundational criteria for deciding Christian identity that make Wessels' interpretation of Christian identity more or less valid than that adopted by National Socialists. Wessels' argument shifts from the historical to the philosophical without, understandably, embarking on a discussion of the complex issues of ethical relativism. What his answer illustrates is the way in which ethics becomes the deciding factor in the question of Christian identity. This problem is one which I shall return to below. Before that I will examine two sets of objections to the notion of ongoing inculturation and the fluidity of Christian identity.

The Historical Jesus

Wessels' thesis is highly controversial. The idea that Christianity has no fixed identity and that local expressions of the religion are constructed by ordinary people challenges deeply held assumptions about the nature of theology. Many would argue that there must be some core or essential element to Christianity which gives it its identity. Some claim that the continuity of identity within Christianity is located in the historical life of Jesus of Nazareth. Bosch hints at this when he proposes that one of the three essential elements of Christian identity was 'the historicity of the humanity of Jesus'. This could mean solely, and merely, that orthodox Christianity was able to resist its opponents by the assertion that Jesus of Nazareth was an historical figure. However, unless certain events can be attributed to the life of this historical figure, such an assertion would be vacuous. So implicit in Bosch's statement is the idea that we can recover and comprehend something of the life of Jesus of Nazareth from the biblical witness. Investigating what this might be has been the task of biblical scholars concerned with the quest for the historical Jesus.

There are two points to be made about the quest for the historical Jesus and which are relevant to our discussion of Christian identity. The first is that it would be far-fetched to suppose that all we know about the historical Jesus is authorial or editorial construction. It would be a very difficult case to argue that Jesus of Nazareth was not an historical figure about whom we have some genuine knowledge. At the same time we have to acknowledge, however, that there is only limited consensus about what Jesus did or said. John Dominic Crossan has written an important study of the historical Jesus. He begins his work by emphasizing the problem of Jesus of Nazareth's diverse identities. Crossan states that within the scholarly community there are a 'number of competent and even eminent scholars producing pictures of Jesus at wide variance with one another'.[25] Crossan cites Daniel J. Harrington's presidential address to the Catholic Biblical Association at Georgetown University on 6 August 1986. The address was later published. Crossan writes:

> In that latter article he gives 'a short description of seven different images of Jesus that have been proposed by scholars in recent years, the differences relating to the different Jewish backgrounds against which they have chosen to locate their image of the historical Jesus'. There is Jesus as a political revolutionary by S.G.F. Brandon (1967), as a magician by Morton Smith (1978), as a Galilean charismatic by Geza Vermes (1981, 1984), as a Galilean rabbi by Bruce Chilton (1984), as a Hillelite or proto-Pharisee by Harvey Falk (1985), as an Essene by Harvey Falk, and as an eschatological prophet by E.P. Sanders (1985).[26]

This does not mean that all these pictures are equally credible within the scholarly biblical community, although they are produced by respected academics. What it does mean, as Crossan himself points out, is that it is 'impossible to avoid the suspicion' that researching the historical Jesus is a 'very safe place to do theology and call it history, to do autobiography and call it biography'. None of the above of course prevents Crossan from adding to the literature on the historical Jesus, nor claiming a more definitive status for his work. He makes his case for greater historicity on the basis of methodological rigour. He argues that his strategy avoids the 'textual looting' he believes leads to such diverse Jesus identities. The methodology employed by Crossan is immensely complex, involving social anthropology and Greco-Roman history, as well as detailed textual criticism, particularly making judgements about chronology, sources and frequency of attestation. The first two parts of his book examine social, cultural, religious, economic and political history around the time of the life of Jesus, based in large part on the work of Josephus. The third part, which focuses on the events surrounding Jesus of Nazareth, is controversial because of a relatively high dependence on extracanonical sources such as the Gospel of Thomas and because of the prominence given to the Sayings Gospel Q. A brief examination of the secondary literature surrounding Crossan's work demonstrates that we are still some way away from reaching consensus about the teachings and activities of Jesus of Nazareth. It could be that the disputes will at some point in the future be sufficiently resolved for us to posit a core set of teachings and actions attributable to Jesus. These could form the basis of a fixed, persistent Christian identity. But to reach such a point we probably need to make discoveries as yet unimagined. Until then, the quest for the historical Jesus does not take us any closer to resolving the problem of different Christian identities; in fact, if anything it increases the problem by generating plural versions of the historical Jesus.

It may be that even if the identity of Jesus of Nazareth cannot be established with any certainty, there is common to all Christians the belief that 'Jesus is Lord'. A simple statement like this will be a focus for unity. Likewise, a belief in the importance of the Church or the centrality of revelation for Christian faith should provide a core belief which is shared by all Christians. However, even this idea has problems. These are highlighted by the work of Professor Dennis Nineham. Nineham studied the Christian beliefs and practices of tenth-century Franks. His purpose was to examine my question, namely: Does religion change in different cultural and historical locations? His conclusions are stark. Nineham argues that what has been meant by the terms 'Christian' and 'Christianity' is so divergent socially, historically and culturally as to describe more than one set of religious beliefs.[27]

The straightforward statement 'Jesus is Lord' illustrates why this is so. Tenth-century Franks had a very sheltered, short and brutal life. They tended to live in one place, their home village, and be subject to all sorts of forces that were beyond their control and understanding. Disease was common and dangerous. Frequently crops would fail and hunger and even starvation would follow. They could be subject to the imposition of taxes to pay for wars whose purpose and origin they did not know or understand. They could also be conscripted into the army required to fight these wars.

The feudal society for tenth-century Franks was rigid and hierarchical. The reigning monarch was a distant figure. The local nobility or gentry were the only means of access to the monarchy should that ever be required. But local gentry could also act in an arbitrary and brutal manner by imposing the taxes or conscripting the men required to fight the King's wars. A lord would visit a village to demand payment or conscript men. Peasants in villages had no comprehension of the economic forces or political affairs that led to the need for more money or soldiers. What this meant was that when tenth-century Franks thought about the word 'lord' then they envisaged an arbitrary, dangerous, brutal and fearsome figure. Lords were to be appeased, pleaded with or avoided. Contact with a lord would usually result in something bad happening, a form of punishment.

What this meant was that when Jesus was described as 'Lord', then the image which had meaning was of a fearsome figure. It was of a person who would judge and punish and who had to be appeased to avoid the worst excesses of damnation. To say 'Jesus is Lord' was to conjure up a brutal, dreaded person who could inflict pain and whose ways were entirely mysterious. The contrast Nineham then makes is with twentieth-century Western evangelicals. They also proclaim their belief that Jesus is Lord. However, they mean something very different. For evangelicals, Jesus is a personal friend. He is a guide and comfort, even a holy, spiritual lover. The image of Jesus' lordship is one of warmth and gracious mercy. 'Lordship' means a close, personal loving relationship, the saviour friend. The contrast with the tenth-century Franks could not be more dramatic. The same phrase has polar opposite meanings. What this means is that even when the same language is being used and is expected to provide continuity in Christianity, in fact different identities are being discussed.

This argument is very similar to Wessels. What is important is the way in which the new religion is received. This can mean how it relates to previous religious beliefs and practices. Or it can refer to the way in which meaning is made in the particular social and cultural setting. In either case, when the cultures and societies are different, as they must be, then what is meant by the religious language or metaphor will change.

If it is the case, as I am arguing, that Christianity is in some ways immersed into the culture in which it enters, the question arises of how Christianity can be counter-cultural. That is, how can Christianity as a set of beliefs and principles challenge the predominant values of the society in which it finds itself? This question was asked sharply in missionary circles by Bishop Lesslie Newbigin.[28] It has also been the focus of much discussion in other theological and philosophical disciplines, not least of which is ethics. Newbigin spent the majority of his life as a Christian missionary in India. On his retirement from this work, he returned to England and was shocked by the society he encountered. This led him to write a series of books critiquing Western society from a Christian perspective. He argued that there had to be a core identity to the Christian religion which was able to transcend cultures.

This core identity, the Gospel Message, challenged society, in particular Western society. Newbigin's historical arguments in favour of a core Christian identity are weak. However, his work does raise the question of how Christianity can challenge a culture if it is itself the product of integration with that culture. Where does the critical voice come from?

At this point it is important to note that there is not one expression of Christianity. Christianity, from the days of the apostle Paul, has had many different identities. This is well known and does not in itself mean that there is no core Christian identity which is a part of each of these separate expressions of the faith. However, what it does mean is that it is possible for Christianity to adopt different forms. There are clear differences between liberal Protestant and Black Pentecostal Christianity, as well as between African Pentecostalism and Latin American Roman Catholicism. Right-wing Southern Baptists from the US bear little resemblance to the majority of British Anglicans. These differences are not only differences between nations and cultures, they are also differences within cultures. Christianity is able to integrate, transform and be transformed by different aspects of one society's cultures. What this can then lead to is a prophetic Christian voice within a culture. But this is not a culturally neutral or separate Christianity critiquing the values and principles of a society. Rather, it is one form of Christianity, having integrated with a minority culture, critiquing the dominant culture of the society. This dominant culture will often have its own Christian apologists. So the Christian prophetic critique of a society can become an internal theological debate, as well as a clash of politics and cultures. Something like the civil rights movement in the USA illustrates the point very well. But equally, so does the liberal left-of-centre critique by the Church of the Bush administration. It is one culturally integrated Christianity critiquing a culture which is not its own. In relation to Newbigin's argument, it means there does not have to be a separate Christian identity so that a society or culture can be critiqued. In fact, what frequently happens is

that Christianity is able to ally itself with a minority culture
and thereby sanction that culture's politics.

The quest for the historical Jesus is an attempt to undo the
barriers erected by history. It seeks to eradicate the gulf
between ourselves and alien cultures, religions, politics and
social norms. It is an attempt to harmonize discordant lan-
guages so that we can know what was originally meant, even if
it was said and done at times and in places of which we cannot
conceive. The danger with the quest is that it reduces the
listener, the recipient of the new story, to the role of a cipher.
It assumes no cultural, religious or linguistic framework into
which new information is to be imparted. But this of course is
never the case. The recipients of a new set of beliefs or values
will compare what is heard with what they already know. More
than this, they will utilize their previous knowledge to make
sense of the new information being transmitted. It is this
process of making meaning, whereby the new is heard through
the ears of the old, which ensures the fluidity of Christian
identity in history. When people in the Hellenistic world heard
about Jesus, they asked themselves, as a tool for understanding, who does this remind us of, who do we know already who
can help us make sense of this mysterious figure? This process
of making meaning has been examined in some detail by Anton
Wessels. It is his idea of ongoing inculturation which shows
how, when Christianity crosses national and cultural borders,
it is transformed. Mission works through a process of adopting
what is resilient within an indigenous culture and transforming it into Christian belief and practice. As this happens, so
the Christianity itself is transformed. The tools of this
process are ordinary people. It is ordinary people who reinvent
Christianity. They did it in the earliest days of the faith and
they continue to do it today.

Chapter Five

Churchgoing and Pilgrimage in the Middle Ages

In this chapter and the next I shall investigate Christian belief and practice during the Middle Ages. The purpose of the investigation is to deepen our understanding of the religious identity of Western secular society. I shall argue that in significant ways religious life in contemporary society is a reversion to medieval Christian beliefs and practice. The exception to this argument is the role played by Christianity as the scientific technology of the Middle Ages. This role has been taken over by secular natural sciences, especially medical science. But in other important ways, what happened in the medieval period is being repeated in Western society today. As such, the Middle Ages provide valuable insights into contemporary religious life.

There is a persistent notion that Western history progresses relentlessly towards increasing secularism. This account of history begins with the crude anthropomorphism of the Greek and Roman gods. This develops into a more theologically and philosophically sophisticated monotheism. A shift in direction towards humanism occurred with the Renaissance before the triumph of the Enlightenment. At the Enlightenment, scientific thought and reason swept away the old superstitions of religion. The final triumph of science and reason depends on education and, increasingly today in the West, the ability of liberals to resist the political power of religious conservatives, be they Christian or Muslim. In this book I am arguing for a different account of humanity's religious history. Rather than think in terms of linear progression, we should be thinking in terms of a succession of peaks and troughs. There are periods of intense religious activity. I have highlighted the Victorian era as of especial importance, but the Reformation is another obvious example, as is the early spread of Christianity. Then there are periods of equilibrium or calm. The late medieval Church is one illustration of a calmer period, as is contemporary Western society. This does not mean nothing religious is happening – clearly a lot is – but it is not as dramatic or universal a phenomenon as those times of intense religious activity. In other words, the periods of equilibrium are a reversion to normality when humans conduct their affairs in a typical manner. The danger is that we interpret these periods of return to religious normality as something new, such as secularism, or something corrupt, such as the pre-Reformation Church. Such an interpretation requires a belief in the exceptional irreligious condition of contemporary Western humanity. It is more straightforward to begin from the premise that people are religiously the same throughout history. Essentially they will behave and believe in the same sort of ways. The local context and social and political movements will add some colour to the picture. But overall, people are not changing so significantly that they go from being religious to leaving religion behind. The task is to compare the right periods with each other.

This chapter will investigate two important areas of comparison between the contemporary and medieval West. The first is the contentious issue of churchgoing. How universal was church attendance in the Middle Ages? Some argue that it was an almost universal phenomenon, whilst others suggest that it was infrequent. The problem is the disputed nature of the evidence, a problem I shall examine below. The second area for examination is the place of supernatural belief within medieval society. For those who want to argue that contemporary society is secular, the decline in belief in spirits and demons is a fundamental part of their case. This means we need to explore the role played by belief in the supernatural world during the Middle Ages.

The difficulty with understanding the scope and nature of Christian belief and practice in the medieval era is that it is a disputed area amongst historians. The key question is the state of the Church prior to the Reformation. The traditional picture is of a Church racked by abuses and in need of change. The clergy were ignorant and ill-educated, frequently absent from their parishes or dioceses and corrupt. Wealthy bishops jockeyed for favour at court, whilst poorly paid curates neglected the spiritual and pastoral welfare of their parishioners. Local clergy, with a few honourable exceptions, could not name the author of the Lord's Prayer, understand the Latin they spoke each week at Mass, or recite the Ten Commandments. Pluralism, the acquisition of more than one parish or diocese, was rife and political skill not godliness was the path to ecclesiastical preferment. The majority of lay people were superstitious, illiterate and, unsurprisingly given the state of the clergy, entirely ignorant of basic Christian teaching. The boundaries between popular Christianity, paganism and magic were blurred to the point at which it was not clear where one began and the other ended.

That everyone went to church was not in itself necessarily to be welcomed. Parishioners might be drunk, liable to fight with their neighbours, gossip, conduct licit or illicit romances, trade goods, arrange or, more amazingly, watch cockfights and heckle any preacher brave enough to request attention. In fact, medieval people seemed determined to do anything in church except what they were supposed to, namely worship God. Priests stood at the east end of the church facing away from the congregation, separated by a Rood screen, mumbling the mass in Latin. People usually only received communion at Easter and then just the Host. Congregations were required to observe but not participate in a ceremony that made little sense to them or the priests who conducted it. Such a Church was, not surprisingly, ripe for and, by the sixteenth century, subject to dramatic theological and spiritual reformation, beginning in Germany and spreading throughout Europe.

Although this is the traditional image of the pre-Reformation Church, recently there has been some considerable revisionist scholarship. Leading the way is Eamon Duffy and his magisterial work *The Stripping of the Altars*.[1] Duffy and others argue that we have inherited a false picture of popular spirituality in the fifteenth and sixteenth century. In fact, Christianity was alive and meaningful in all sections of society. The clergy and laity were better educated than we usually imagine and through preaching and devotional texts people had a faith that informed their lives. People were willing to undertake the sacrifice of pilgrimage, sometimes involving long and dangerous journeys abroad, and were faithful supporters of the mass through weekly and in some cases daily attendance. Saints were prayed to and relics were venerated. The English Reformation of Henry VIII was not a long-awaited popular revival, casting aside a corrupt, despised Church, but a top-down imposition by a political and theological elite. The persistence of pre-Reformation rituals and ceremonies during the mid and later Tudor period in England bear witness to the importance of medieval Christianity amongst the population. Parishes would either defy an admittedly weak central government or only introduce reforms at the very last moment and under duress. The consensus within recent scholarship is that the traditional picture of the medieval Church was too dependent on the propaganda of the reformers and that its extremes need to be refined. It is wrong to believe that everything about the Church in the Middle Ages was corrupt. This is after all the Church of Thomas Aquinas, St Francis, Julian of Norwich and St Benedict, to name but an illustrious few.

It is the conflict between these two pictures which must warn us to tread carefully. What we shall find is something between the two extremes. Churches were neither full nor empty. What was crucial often were local factors, a responsible priest, a nearby Church, a community feeling threatened by forces it could not comprehend. These factors we shall examine below. However, before I look in detail at the discussion, it is necessary to clarify two important questions. The first is: What do we mean by 'Middle Ages'? Precisely which period is being described? This is important because of the variations in the state of the Church at different periods in its history. The second question is: What evidence do we have of Christian life in the relevant period? This is significant because it is problems with the evidence which have led to the different interpretation of the extent and nature of Christianity.

Defining the Middle Ages

What do we mean when we say 'Middle Ages' or 'medieval period'? The division of history into periods can be a very general and arbitrary task. The broadest definition of the Middle Ages is from 700 CE, roughly the end of the Roman Empire, until 1500 CE and the break down of the Church–state hegemony in the West. This is a time span of some 800 years. It is therefore in need of some more refined division if it is to make sense. R.W. Southern divides the medieval period into three: 700–1050, 1050–1300 and 1300–1550.[2] In the first period the West was weak. People were poor, population numbers were low, society was predominantly rural and most people subject to famine and plague. Christianity was new to many parts of Europe and relatively weak. In terms of church attendance, many would have been unlikely or unable to go, because no Christian communities existed in their local vicinity. Journeys to church would have been too long and hazardous to be worth the effort and there were few local clergy able to enforce or promote attendance.

The second period, 1050–1300, was a time of Western economic growth and expansion. Western Europe was able to assert itself on the back of increased prosperity. A key indicator of economic growth was the development of new rural communities alongside the significant reversal of urban decline. The era spurned the need for a variety of specialist activities. Expertise was required to solve the complex problems for which ritual was no longer an adequate solution. Towering above the trade guilds and government administrations developed during this period was the Church's bureaucracy and hierarchy. The Church became the expert in all matters spiritual and many things temporal. And by 'Church' was meant the clerical elite as distinct from lay people and secular lay rulers. Southern states: 'The ecclesiastical organization elaborated between 1050 and 1300 was the most splendid system, both theoretically and practically, that the church has ever known.' The papacy was in its pomp. However, paradoxically the system, whilst revealing the Church at its strongest, also demonstrated the inherent weakness of the clergy. The Church had no effective means of enforcing its edicts in the face of secular opinion, especially when this was led by the governing classes. The symbolic last stand of the papacy came during this period over the issue of taxation. In theory, ecclesiastical revenue could only be taxed with clerical consent. In 1296, Pope Boniface VIII attempted to enforce this law by insisting on papal agreement before Church income could be taxed. In reality, secular rulers were able to tax ecclesiastical income almost at will. Within months Boniface was forced to back down, explain the decree away and allow the effective continuation of a system which recognized that ultimate power lay with secular rulers. Much historical scholarship has explored this second period. It has largely focused on the power of the Papacy and its relations with secular rulers. What is missing is much evidence of popular Christian beliefs and practices. There is far more evidence of popular Christianity in the third period Southern identifies. For that reason I shall focus my discussions on the period 1300–1550.

Southern calls the third period, from 1300 to 1550, the 'Age of Unrest'. This is with a view to the subsequent events of the European Reformation and its enormous ecclesiastical and political change. During this period the papacy was a weakened force and one which tended towards theological and political conservatism. Secular rulers shared the desire for social and political stability. However, this stability was under threat. The major factor fermenting unrest was the growth of urban populations. This was not new, but it was of a new order after 1300. For example, in Florence the population grew from about 10,000 to 30,000 in the 100 years prior to 1300. However, in the 45 years after 1300 it rose by 90,000 to 120,000. The consequence of the growth was social and political radicalism. This Southern attributes to human nature. Where one person in a mainly self-contained rural community might learn to keep quiet about more radical notions for fear of being ostracized, in a city they were liable to find like-minded friends. The courage of a few with shared beliefs is then more likely to become a political movement supported by larger numbers. Such a movement can be easily radicalized by short-term economic crises or incidents of religious fervour. It is no surprise that in this climate political and ecclesiastical authorities favoured stability.

It is from this third period that we have most evidence about the religious beliefs and behaviour of people in the Middle Ages. For this reason I shall focus on the late Middle Ages as my period of comparison with contemporary religious behaviour. But this is not exclusive. I shall not neglect evidence from other periods when this is available and can be usefully employed.

The evidence we have for religious beliefs and practices at the end of the medieval period is richer than for any time previously, but it is still not substantial. It does not compare with what we have from the Victorian era. Records from the last 150 years are by no means perfect. There are problems with the survey data. It is well known that more people claim to attend church in the USA than can reasonably be fitted into the available buildings. But compared with the late medieval period, we have a veritable treasure trove of information. There were no sociological studies of religious movements, churches or sects in the Middle Ages. We have no surveys of the general population from which to begin discussing likely patterns of behaviour or belief. Instead, the evidence is eclectic and fragmentary. Eamon Duffy provides a useful summary of the evidence he drew upon for his study of England between 1400 and 1580. He uses the term 'traditional religion' where I have employed the concept of popular religion. Duffy states:

> In attempting to delineate the character of that traditional religion I have drawn on a wide variety of sources, from liturgical books to painted images, from saints' lives and devotional treatises to play texts, and from churchwarden's accounts and ecclesiastical court records to personal commonplace books and wills. I have also drawn on a good deal of local and parochial material, especially on the riches of the church in East Anglia, for my non-documentary evidence, but, somewhat unfashionably this is not a regional study.[3]

Duffy is right to say that a lot of recent studies have focused on local churches. When general evidence is so sparse then it makes sense to find out as much as possible about a specific location from a wide range of sources. Such work is time consuming, but provides a fuller picture than might otherwise be possible. Interestingly, this is a technique employed by scholars examining more recent Church life.[4] Duffy's use of non-textual sources is a method employed by others. Rosalind and Christopher Brooke's study of popular religion in the period from 1000 to 1300 recognizes that most lay people were illiterate, and therefore it is buildings and paintings which will tell us most about their religion.[5] Of the evidence Duffy cites, it is perhaps wills, court records and churchwarden's accounts which figure most frequently in the work of other scholars. Last wills and testaments tell us about the priorities of people at the time of their death and so have an understandable focus on the next life. But the fear of hell and purgatory was very real. That death was so common and early death a likelihood means this is probably a good reflection of the daily concerns of people. Churchwarden's accounts tell us what the laity prioritized financially in the part of the Church for which they had responsibility. It is by looking at spending priorities that we can deduce some of the religious and spiritual concerns of lay people. The court records are interesting because they illustrate the extent of religious non-conformity during the period. They relate the crimes of those who broke Church laws. It is from these records that we get a sense of what was happening in church which shouldn't have been. Duffy also draws on what he calls the personal commonplace books of individuals. These include extracts of prayers and texts to support a private devotional life. They often include instructions on what to pray or meditate upon at various stages of the mass. Duffy is keen to highlight the devotion of lay people as part of his argument that the pre-Reformation Church was in far better health than has previously been supposed. As such, these texts are a good antidote to the court records, which highlight the opposite.

In addition to the sources Duffy mentions, it is also important to highlight the records of miracles at shrines. These were written by monks assigned to the task and described the miracles attributed to the saints whose relics were kept at the shrine. The records served a financial and ecclesiastical function in promoting the efficacy of the particular saint. But this said, they should not be treated entirely sceptically, as efforts were made to check the validity of claimed cures. One of the most important shrines from this period was that of St Thomas Beckett at Canterbury. Two monks, Benedict of Canterbury and William of Canterbury, recorded the miracles, leaving us a wealth of data about the healings attributed to the saint.

It is certainly the case that the evidence for this period could be better, but there is much that can inform our understanding of the period. What is also required is an interpretation of the evidence so that some of the more glaring omissions can be filled. There has been a tendency to interpret the evidence by arguing that either churches were empty or churches were full. We shall tread a path between these two extremes.

Church Attendance in the Middle Ages

Before I discuss who went to church and what they did there, it is important to understand something of the social and economic conditions of the Middle Ages. This will help comprehension of why religious life took the form it did. I am focusing mainly on England so that I can compare my conclusions with what I have already said about contemporary UK society. What becomes apparent, unsurprisingly, is that there are considerable social and economic differences between contemporary and medieval society.

The first significant difference between contemporary and medieval society is population numbers. In 1500 the population of England and Wales was a mere 2.5 million, rising to 5.5 million by 1700.[6] Most of the population lived in the countryside, as much as 80 per cent by the late seventeenth century. Cities were much smaller than we are used to today, even London, although this stood out as by far the largest. Society was highly stratified, with between a third and a half living at or near subsistence levels. Nutrition was universally atrocious. The poor were subject to a food supply that was extremely precarious: one in six harvests are thought to have failed. The wealthy had a better supply but tended to consume a diet rich in meat. Vegetables were perceived to be poor people's food. Life expectancy was low, even for the nobility, and infant mortality rates were high. Thirty-six of every 100 died in the first six years. The bubonic plague was a persistent and real threat which wiped out large numbers of the population swiftly and brutally. No one understood its causes. Medicine was at best haphazard and at worst positively dangerous. All but the wealthiest were spared the medical lottery, because it was well beyond their financial means. The poor turned to family remedies and wise women for cures, as well as the Church. Those sufficiently robust and resilient to survive the plague, the terrible diet and the attentions of the medical profession lived in fear of fire. It was a constant threat. Buildings, heated by domestic fires and lit by candles, were easily ignited and almost impossible to extinguish. There was no meaningful insurance and so a wealthy family could be reduced to poverty over one combustible night. Professor Keith Thomas comments that it is no surprise that people sort solace in beer and later tobacco, although these were hardly comforts liable to reduce the risk of fire or improve general health. The earliest figures suggest that, for every man, woman and child in the population, 40 gallons of beer a year were consumed, or about a pint a day. Given that children would not be drinking their fair share and the women drank less, this meant some men were consuming a lot of beer. No wonder some were drunk in church – how could they not be.

Life in the late Middle Ages was fragile, vulnerable, difficult and frequently excruciatingly painful. Some accounts of healing miracles at shrines are so gory and disgusting they are difficult to read. For example, one poor woman's cure was described this way:

> While she prayed she suffered more bitterly than before and she thought [she heard] many twigs being snapped in pieces inside her head. She asked those standing around whether they heard the noise in her head. But while she was being racked this way, she cried out to the Lord and he heard her. For as she shouted, a great deal of matter flowed out of her ears, as if some inner abscess had ruptured. The matter was followed by blood, and the blood by the gift [of the return] of her lost hearing.[7]

There is a question here of whether the cure was worth the medicine. If ever a society needed a national health service this was it. But none existed outside of popular wisdom and the ministrations of the Church.

It is bearing in mind this social, economic and medical context that we can investigate the Christian belief and practice of the time. The first question concerns the vexed subject of churchgoing. Did everyone go to church and, equally

as pertinent, what did they do when they got there? In relation
to the first point, we can be certain that everyone was legally
required to go to church. There is little doubt about this. The
question is whether this was a law more honoured in the breach
than fulfilment. Those who argue that the pre-Reformation
Church was spiritually strong argue that attendance was the
norm and reflected the real place of Christian faith in people's
lives. Duffy begins his examination of popular spirituality with
the practices linked to the Christian liturgical year. He argues
that the Church's festivals and celebrations, as well as fasts and
penances, shaped the worldview of medieval society. The
Church provided the landscape through which life was understood. In this cultural context the minimum requirement was
'regular and sober attendance at matins, Mass, and evensong on
Sundays and feasts, and annual confession and communion at
Easter'. Did people do this? Duffy states that 'Ecclesiastical law
and the vigilance of bishop, archdeacon, and parson' would
have ensured regular attendance.[8] In fact, Duffy goes further
and argues that 'many lay people, perhaps even most of them,
attended Mass on some weekdays'.[9] The first piece of evidence
for such devotion is the architecture of medieval churches.
Large cathedrals and even small local churches had side altars
for the saying of guild and chantry masses. A small church like
that at Wellingham, only 16 feet wide, had an additional 'altar
pushed up against the south screen'. These additional altars
were required for the liturgical practices of the laity. Personal
piety is also apparent in some written evidence. A major source
for Duffy is *The Book of Margery Kempe*. Kempe, a pious woman,
received communion on a weekly basis. This was regarded as an
ostentatious show of piety which rankled with her neighbours.[10] But for Duffy and many of the revisionist Reformation
scholars, her devotion is a sign that church attendance was a not
merely a regular requirement but also a reality. The Christian
faith had a real place in individual lives and local communities.

The evidence for the opposite point of view is equally
sketchy. In the earliest part of the Middle Ages, it is clear there
were not enough churches in the locality for everyone to

attend. The mendicant orders, itinerant friars, of the thirteenth century and afterwards sought to promote church attendance but met with resistance. It was their complaint that 'apprentices played football while they should have been at Mass, while menservants lounged and gossiped outside churches but seldom entered them'.[11] Keith Thomas argues that the problem of church size and location remained into the later Middle Ages and Reformation periods. Because of population shifts, churches were often located in the wrong place or were too small for a newly formed community. In addition, Thomas argues that social class made a significant difference to attendance. It was a constant fault of the poor that they never came to weekly Mass. They probably did take advantage of the rites of baptism and burial, but beyond that attendance was intermittent or rare. In some cases their absence was to be desired as there was a fear that poor people carried the plague on their persons.

Nor was the situation ideal amongst the wealthier classes. We have records of the excuses more established members of the community made for non-attendance at Church. These included illness, necessary work to be undertaken, fear of being arrested for bad debts and excommunication. Of the latter group, Thomas suggests this may have amounted to some 15 per cent of the population, a sign of the flagging authority of ecclesiastical courts. What this resulted in was a situation far from the legal ideal. Thomas wrote that:

> In 1540–52 it was said that not half the communicants in the parish of St Giles, Colchester, went to Church on Sundays and holidays; in 1633 there were twelve hundred absentees at Easter communion in Great Yarmouth. Many contemporaries echoed the complaint of the Jacobean preacher who said that there were 'sometimes not half the people in a parish present at holy exercises upon the Sabbath day, so hard a thing is it to draw them to the means of their salvation'. It really was a case of two or three persons gathered together in

God's name, wrote a pamphleteer in 1635; sometimes there were more pillars in church than people. In Winchester in 1656 the almsmen had to be forced into church by the threat of being denied poor relief if they stayed away.[12]

Although some of these illustrations come from the period after the one under discussion, there is no reason to suppose the situation was any better earlier. It could well have been worse, as in the earlier period there was less likely to be as strong ecclesiastical control as later.

Before we try and assess this contradictory evidence, it is important to examine the supplementary question of what people did if and when they came to church. The first thing that will be apparent is that attending church in the Middle Ages bears little resemblance to the contemporary Western experience. Whereas modern Western services frequently aim to be communal and participative and have an ethos of being with and by the people, medieval liturgy was distant and the preserve of the priest. Masses in the Middle Ages were done by the priest and for the people. The priest was separated from the people by the physicality of the Rood screen, by the Latin of the mass and by a theology which emphasized the special status of the Host. At the mass the elements of bread and wine were transformed into the body and blood of Christ. It was the moment at which heaven and earth touched each other. There is a consensus that normally most people did not receive the Host each Sunday. It was too dangerous an activity to receive communion when still in a state of sin. Making communion happened once a year at Easter after personal confession during Holy Week. Instead, the centre and spiritual focus of the weekly service was the elevation and observation of the Host by the people. Bells were rung to warn congregations that the Host was about to be elevated, so that they could stop whatever they were doing and see it. Some churches still have peep holes in Rood screens which allowed congregational members a better sighting of the elevated Host. At the moment of elevation, people were often encouraged to recite prayers such as the Lord's Prayer or a hymn to the Virgin Mary. These might be more or less theologically sophisticated depending on the literacy of the congregation. Duffy argues that the more holy regularly, sometimes daily, took advantage of the opportunity of being in the presence of the consecrated bread and wine. This was more normal for the gentry and for royalty who were able to support personal chaplains. It was a means of ensuring protection and good fortune for the day.

The question is: what did people do for the rest of the time in church? Those who want to argue that late medieval religion was devout and real argue that prayers and holy books were read or recited prior to the elevation of the Host. In some cases sermons would be preached. Those priests unable to construct their own words of wisdom could read suitable homilies from collections circulated widely after the advent of printing, but also available beforehand. Duffy argues that, even though the literate and well off would clearly have access to a wider range of devotional material, nevertheless the illiterate and poor could meditate on cheap woodcuts depicting suitable images. This is part of his attempt to refute the idea that a division existed between a small minority of educated and more devout gentry and the majority of the population who were ignorant and irreligious.[13]

The contrasting opinion suggests that almost anything you can imagine except spiritual devotions occurred in church. Local churches were social centres. This meant they were places in which business was conducted. Goods could be bought and sold or bartered. Churches were also places of romance, or at least opportunities to survey potential marriage partners. For example, an Italian woman Alessandra Strozzi wrote to her son in 1465 describing how she had been working hard to secure his future happiness. In her letter to the son Filippo, she wrote:

> I must tell you how, during the *Ave Maria* at the first mass at Santa Liperata, having gone there several times

> on feast mornings to see the Adimari girl as she usually
> goes to that mass, I found the Tanagli girl there. Not
> knowing who she was, I sat on one side of her and had a
> good look at her....[14]

The verdict was that she was very pretty. Where there was business and romance there was also gossip. It seems to be a constant complaint of the more devout that too many people spent too much time in churches gossiping. But if anything, gossiping was the mild end of the spectrum of inappropriate behaviour. Thomas compares the typical congregation with a class of unruly schoolboys. He states: 'Members of the congregation jostled for pews, nudged their neighbours, hawked and spat, knitted, made coarse remarks, told jokes, fell asleep, and even let off guns.'[15] Faced with the prospect of a sermon, it was reported some congregations hastily departed and went home to drink. This might have been preferable for some clergy, as we learn that when congregations stayed they would heckle preachers or complain it was milking time if the preacher went on too long. Once released from church notorious congregations went off to the alehouse, sharing blasphemous jokes and engaging in at best boisterous behaviour. There were the typical complaints about the young and poor, neither of which group knew about or cared for religion and holiness.

The behaviour of the congregations is less surprising when we hear about some of the clergy. Carl Volz recounts some of the experiences of the thirteenth-century Archbishop of Rouen from his visitations in his diocese. The report from February 1248 states:

> We found that the priest of Ruiville was ill-famed with
> the wife of a certain stone carver, and by her is said to
> have had a child; he does not stay in his church, he plays
> ball, and he rides around in a short coat (the garb of
> armed men); the priest of Ribeuf frequents taverns
> and drinks to excess. Simon, the priest of St Just, is
> pugnacious and quarrelsome.[16]

The situation was no better in larger churches; in a visit to one the archbishop found that 'the canons talk and chatter from stall to stall, and across each other, while the divine office is being celebrated. They hasten through the psalms too quickly'. Although this report is taken from the very fringe of the period I am focusing on, it has the advantage that the archbishop's reports can hardly be thought of as Reformers' propaganda. As we have seen from the late Middle Ages, descriptions of drunken, ignorant, illiterate clergy unable to recite the Lord's Prayer or the Ten Commandments, or have even a basic knowledge of Eucharistic theology or salvation history, are legion. No doubt some of these are justified and some apocryphal.

So where does this leave us? Are we to believe the Church of the late Middle Ages was a thriving and holy community, with occasional exceptions, or was it made up of a corrupt, ignorant clergy leading an immoral, spiritually negligent laity? The answer no doubt lies somewhere between these two extremes. It is perhaps not surprising that the evidence we have is of the extremes of behaviour, as this is what would have been noteworthy and recorded for posterity. There would have been cases of remarkable piety and also examples of astonishing immorality and blasphemy. But one can imagine that the majority of medieval religion was more mundane. And it would have depended on local factors. Where the local clergy were diligent, then people may well have been encouraged into church and thought it wise to attend. If a local priest inspired people by his manner of life, again a majority would have wanted to know more and felt attendance at Church was worthwhile. Likewise, absentee clergy or those focused on temporal matters might have found their churches emptier on a Sunday morning. Local landowners could likewise have influenced behaviour either way. The availability of churches and priests in the vicinity would also have been another crucial local factor. If a newly populated area did not have adequate provision then the social pressure to attend Church would have been that much less. Likewise, social pressure would have been less in towns or cities compared with stable rural communities, although in towns more churches would have been available.

Another factor would have been external events. Some preachers blamed outbreaks of the plague on the drunkenness or godlessness of the general population. God punishes those who do not obey holy law. In times of social or economic crisis, more people may well have gone to church in an effort to win divine favour or at least undo whatever harsh judgment and penalty was being inflicted on them. Alternately, in times of prosperity and good health the urge to turn to the divine diminishes. Duffy emphasizes the importance of festivals and pilgrimages when assessing the extent of traditional religious activity. The beating of the bounds was a major communal event, as were the processions at the feast of Corpus Christi. Certainly the church was a major social centre and this may have drawn people into its walls in greater numbers than today. But we have to be careful of such evidence. In contemporary Western society there is widespread celebration of Christmas each year. It dominates television, magazines and newspapers, and is celebrated in schools and workplaces. People have a basic understanding that it is the time when the birth of Christ is remembered. So the evidence, viewed hundreds of years from now, may well suggest a major Christian festival being celebrated each year. But few Church leaders rejoice at the spiritual health of society each December; in fact, quite the opposite. Like their forebears in the Middle Ages they complain that the festival is too drunken and irreverent and that most people are ignorant of its true meaning.

What is clear from the evidence is that medieval society did not run a type of dictatorial totalitarian ecclesiastical state. People were not lined up and counted in and out, with those absent being severely punished. Nor does it seem that the Christian worldview was so ingrained in individuals and society that they came to church each Sunday either out of habit or for fear of eternal damnation. Whatever was the norm, there are enough exceptions to demonstrate that universal belief and practice were not expected or imposed by either ecclesiastical authorities or personal theological nervousness.

One way to cut through the dilemma of churchgoing is to take as our starting point contemporary practice. In the UK today we can say that about 15 per cent of the population take religion seriously, by which I mean they support their local religious community. About 10 per cent entirely reject religious belief and practice as superstitious nonsense. The remaining 75 per cent tend to say they believe in God and will usually call themselves Christian. A good proportion of this 75 per cent, although by no means all, are likely to support the Church at some point in their lives. They might avail themselves of the services of the Church for baptisms, weddings or funerals. And even if they themselves do not use the Church in this way, they will support their family or friends if they do. Some may attend church once at year at Christmas or Easter. The extent to which these numbers hold up depends on local circumstances and recent social history. In the twentieth century, as we have seen, there had been periods when church attendance was higher than now. It is also the case that a village with a poor or negligent clergy person will experience numbers significantly lower than 15 per cent. We can reasonably suppose that medieval devotion mirrors our own times. Some, a very small minority, were anti the Church and probably notorious in their communities. A larger minority were devout and pursued their religion vigorously. The majority were generally sympathetic and supportive. More actually attended church than today, but this was largely due to the social function performed by the church. When they were there it is highly improbable that they were all praying earnestly and meditating on the reform of their lives, any more than a good Christmas dinner demonstrates assent to the doctrine of the Incarnation. Perhaps a good model for comparison is the UK National Health Service. All citizens in the UK belong and pay taxes towards its upkeep. Just about everyone comes into contact with doctors or hospitals at some stage in their lives. This is likely to increase the older one gets. But certain people rarely

seem to need to go to a doctor and others are seeking advice on
a regular basis. Almost universally, health is seen to be an
important issue. It would be a genuine social heresy to suggest
one's health is unimportant. Some, however, go further than
this and are seriously committed to good diet and keeping fit.
Others make little or no effort to exercise or eat well. The
majority are somewhere in between. They could eat better and
exercise more, but they are not careless and neglectful.
Medieval devotion and churchgoing functioned in much the
same way. For the majority, the Church and Christianity were
a presence in their lives to be acknowledged and rarely questioned. But they were not fanatical in either their beliefs or
practices. In this, if we bear in mind the qualification about the
social function performed by the Church, they resemble the
religious commitments of contemporary people in the West.

The Power of the Supernatural in the Middle Ages

Whilst it might be agreed that church attendance was not
universal, nor always especially devout, those who want to
argue that we now live in a secular age highlight the shift away
from belief in the supernatural. In the Middle Ages, people
believed in the power of demons, the healing abilities of relics
and the protection offered by dead saints. In fact, for many
commentators it is saints and shrines which are the essence of
medieval popular religion. The adoration and invocation of
saintly assistance, combined with pilgrimage and the promise
of pilgrimage to shrines, were at the heart of the practice of
Christianity in the Middle Ages and beyond. Compared with
this medieval dialogue with the supernatural, we are a secular
age devoid of any appreciation of the importance of the
afterlife and its continuing influence on our affairs.

Such general assertions are to be taken seriously. We shall see
that in some senses they are correct and an important contrast
should be drawn. But we also need to be aware that the picture
is far more complex than a simple supernatural/natural
dualism might suggest. For example, we should not forget the

70–80 per cent of contemporary Western people who state in surveys that they believe in God. This may well not be an orthodox Christian doctrine of God they are assenting to; in fact, it is a view of the Divine which will be packed full of many quirky and unorthodox beliefs. But when people say they believe in God, they will at least mean something supernatural. Those who want to deny any belief in the supernatural will say they do not believe in God. So one immediate and important qualification to the secular picture of contemporary society is the frequently recorded view that people believe something supernatural exists. It is with similar caution and attention to detail that we need to examine medieval beliefs in the supernatural.

It is fair to say that medieval belief in the supernatural was all-pervasive. It had two elements. The first was the threat to safety and security posed by malevolent spirits. Actions had to be taken to rid the home and local area of demons. One very important community event which had as its aim the banishing of demons from the local community was the Rogationtide procession. It was a community event which everyone had to attend, although that does not mean it was a deeply sacred event. It may be the procession had the same status as the celebration of Christmas, Thanksgiving or even Harvest, a popular festival meaning different things to different people. The purpose of the procession was to drive malevolent spirits out of the parish. To this end banners were carried, bells rung and the litany of the saints sung around the boundaries of the parish. A cross was carried symbolizing the victory of Christ over the devil. At certain points around the parish boundary, portions of the Gospels were read. This would drive out demons from the parish and bring fertility to the fields. Such points were often marked with stone crosses. It has been reported that Rogationtide processions could be the source of inter-parish violence. Neighbouring parishes would seek to prevent processions for fear the demons would be driven out of the processing parish and into their own. Fights are known to have occurred.

The Rogationtide processions were not stand-alone events. They were a major celebration in a culture living permanently in fear of the power of demons. Another important family and community ritual was baptism. The main purpose of baptism was to drive out the devil. It was an exorcism rite. Those not baptized, usually babies, were thought to be denied eternal life, entering instead a sort of limbo which was neither heaven nor hell.

Demons were thought to be especially at large during thunderstorms. Specially blessed candles were lit during storms to ward them off. Likewise, for the same purpose, church bells were rung. At the point of death demons were thought to be particularly active, seeking to snatch the soul at the last moment for the devil and hell. Artwork depicting deathbed scenes show demons circulating around the unfortunate patient. A frequent prayer of the living as well as the dying was that they would have enough time for a final confession, communion and the last rites administered by a priest. One of the problems of clerical absenteeism was that no priest was sufficiently local to be available at short notice should they be required for the last rites. At the point of birth and the moment of death, and all times in between, misfortune and disaster were thought to be the product of the malevolent spirits that clustered in the medieval atmosphere like flies on a hot day. Supernatural demons were to be ignored at your peril.

If demons were the source of misfortune and disaster, then protection and good health came from the saints and their relics. The expectation was that if a saint was honoured in some way, then a form of contract had been entered into by which the saint would use their supernatural power or influence to protect or cure the individual. Saints could be local and thereby sympathetic to their fellow citizen, or they might have expertize in a particular illness or misfortune. In England, St Thomas (Beckett) was popular in Kent, whilst St Richard of Chichester had a following in Sussex and the Thames Valley, Thomas Cantilupe in Hereford and the West Midlands, and

Etheldreda in East Anglia.[17] Saints were usually expected to be particularly effective if they had had some personal experience of the misfortune affecting the supplicant. Of these the best is St Apollonia, of whom legend says her teeth were extracted as part of the torture prior to her martyrdom. She was naturally therefore sympathetic to toothache. Other specialists are listed by Duffy and included 'Barbara and Katherine in child-birth and against sudden and unprepared death, Anthony against ergotism, Roche and Sebastian against the plague, Erasmus against intestinal disorders, Master John Schorne or St Petronilla against the ague'.[18]

Individuals in trouble or ill-health would promise a pilgrim-age to the shrine of the saint if a cure was effected. Or they would pledge a measure of string, usually a body length, to act as a wick for a candle which would be donated at the saint's shrine. Another pledge at times of crisis was to bend a coin. The bending of the coin was a sign that it would become an offering to the saint. Sometimes the act of bending the coin or pledging the string would be enough for a cure to be effected or for the particular crisis to end. Sailors in storms might vow to undertake pilgrimages and make offerings if they were safely returned to harbour. The records we have show that these vows were taken very seriously and conscientiously fulfilled on return to dry land. If for some reason pilgrimage vows were not fulfilled, then the last will and testament of an individual would leave sufficient funds for one to be carried out by proxy. A proxy pilgrimage might also be organized by a living person if for some reason they were unable or unwilling to embark on the requisite journey.

The shrine of a saint would contain some part of their body or special item of clothing. These relics had been part of Church life for centuries. Relics had been placed in the thrones of monarchs and emperors. They were used when political leaders made pacts. It was Harold's crime that the promise he broke to William the Conqueror was sworn on holy relics. Relics could also feature in criminal charges as a test of inno-cence or as a check against perjury. But though relics performed these political and judicial functions, it was their healing powers that were most important in the late Middle Ages.

We noted earlier healing powers attributed to St Thomas Becket at Canterbury, as recorded by the two monks Benedict and William. People were cured of all sorts of maladies and by all sorts of methods. Sight could be restored, aches and pains removed, backs straightened, hearing returned, internal disorders cured and mental health reinstated. Cures could be effected immediately or after a supplicant had returned home and waited many months. They might be total or partial, and they could be after a period of great suffering and pain or quick and easy. Perhaps the most spectacular was the restoring to life of the deceased. A child might have drowned or an individual fallen from a height or been run over by a cart. These victims were presumed dead until the intervention of the saint, usually on the promise of a pilgrimage or offering.

Efforts were made to verify accounts of healing miracles. We should not think that such accounts were a result of the credulous encouraging of the gullible. There was a social hierarchy to the miracles. If the story of a miracle came from the nobility or the gentry, then it was treated as true and credible. The same would be true if the upper classes acted as witness. Where the upper classes were not involved, then witnesses would be sought to verify the story of the healed individual. Some evidence of the changed condition of the person would be required and we can suppose that not all accounts could fulfil these criteria. So stories were not constructed at will or with no regard to the truth. This begs a question: namely, what was it that was really happening during these recorded cures?

The first thing to note is that supplication to the saint was not the only effort made to save an individual. Often it would be combined with other forms of health care, or in fact be the last resort of the desperate after a long process of trying to find a cure. This means a number of factors, dismissed in favour of the intervention of the saint, may well have actually affected a change in the individual's condition. When a cure happens some time after the visit to a shrine, then a change in

n in this section is the predominance of a belief in the
tural. Medieval society's fear of demons and reliance
acle cures suggests that a supernatural worldview was
ant. In one sense this is true. The evidence suggests that
as a very particular type of supernatural worldview.
n best be thought of as a technological functional
rnaturalism. Medieval society was beset by events and
nomena that they, we now realize, did not properly under-
d. This ranged from natural phenomena such as thunder
rms to illnesses caused by poor diet, bad sanitation and
ntal health problems. Medieval people sought to explain
d cope with these problems by attributing them to malign
irits and enlisting the aid of benevolent supernatural friends
the saints. As such, they created what we would think of as
technology of the supernatural. The world of demons and
saints is the equivalent of our world of medicine, meteorology
and science. It is not preposterous to suggest that medicine has
a history that goes back to the cures effected by pilgrimages to
holy shrines.

What this means is that when it is argued that we no longer
have the supernatural worldview of the Middle Ages, then
what we are saying in particular is that our science, and especially our medical science, no longer depends on appeals to
saints or the ejection of demons. Put another way, we are saying that our technology now depends on our own medical
resources rather than the mysterious intervention of the
supernatural. The shrines of the medieval Church have been
replaced by hospitals and doctors' surgeries, whilst pilgrimages are now merely the attempt to get an appointment with
a local physician. Similarly, the success or failure of crops or
sea voyages or commercial enterprises can be predicted or
explained by human sciences.

Our analysis of this shift in human understanding and
culture is of course not new, but the implications for understanding the history of secularism are. During the Middle
Ages we had a society which employed some of its own human
technology, for example the popular cures suggested by wise

diet, such as an improvement i.
period of rest may well have affec
itself might have removed the su
the problem if it was caused by un
dirty food and water. In additior
suppose the medieval assessment of
modern medical diagnosis. Clearly, s
dead would not be thought so today. We
raised to life by the intervention of St T
falling in a quarry pool was not actually
recovered after being hung upside down ¿
of his feet beaten, spending the night on ¿
and then having his front teeth broken so he
water, is testament to an eight-year-old's resil
and the local priest and many others, swore
who recorded the miracle that the boy was dea
our doubts.[19] It is also worth noting that not al
answered favourably. We can assume that many
came to try for a cure went away disappointed. O
had initial periods when their reputation grew beca
success of requests for cures. This would then die
the next shrine would be to the fore. If many people
been disappointed in their first attempt, then they wo
have needed to seek the aid of the newest saint to hit the
lines. The Church suggested a number of reasons why
did not work. It may be something was at fault with
supplicant. They had a secret sin, a lack of faith or had
fully fulfilled their vow or promise. This would be known
the saint. Or there may have been reasons well beyond th
understanding of people, but known to God and God alone.
That failed cures were a fact of life is exemplified by the
numbers who died from the plague. But the seeming failure did
not undermine or diminish the hope of the sick. They were no
doubt desperate. They had few alternatives and what alternatives existed were as equally haphazard and unreliable.

Whilst the question of validity is one that immediately
arises when miracle cures are discussed, the important

women, but depended mainly on the supernatural as an explanation of a world we now know they did not understand. Contemporary Western society has shifted the balance. Western citizens depend mainly on human technology for healing and cures. This does not mean there is no place for the supernatural. The despairing and desperate, as well as the faithful, will seek divine help and make pacts or deals. But mainly we depend on technology and medical science. In other words, the medieval place and role of religious belief has been overtaken by science. What is interesting is that in the meantime religious belief has not gone away. In fact, paradoxically the age of scientific vigour in the West, the Victorian era, was also the time of renewed Christian commitment. It is right to argue that we no longer depend on the supernatural for what are now scientific problems. But a sense of the supernatural is still apparent in society. The end of the technological function of religion has not meant the end of belief in God. Rather, the latter is resilient and attracts many of the scientists and medical practitioners who have supposedly usurped its place.

In this chapter I have investigated the place of Christianity in the Middle Ages. I began with the negatives. Those who suggest a long-term secularization of the West argue that during the Middle Ages people almost universally went to church. In addition, their lives were dominated by a supernatural worldview. In response, I have suggested two important qualifications to this picture. First, it is very doubtful that everyone went to church; in fact, we can reasonably argue that large sections of the population did not go, especially the poor. Furthermore, those who were there were not necessarily or especially devout. Second, the general comment that the West no longer possesses the supernatural worldview of the Middle Ages has had to be refined. The specific role played by supernatural belief, the explanation and manipulation of natural phenomena such as disease and storms, is what has been lost. This is a limited function now undertaken by science and technology. Despite the shift in role we have not had a concurrent reduction in belief in God and, in some cases since the advent of modern science, there have been periods of increased religious belief and activity. What this suggests is that, first, Christianity is able to mutate as the local context in which it exists changes. Second, the resilience or otherwise of the Christian faith in Western society is not directly related to the prevalence of a medieval supernatural worldview. In fact, we can speculate that the basic model of part human technology and part appeal to the supernatural remains. What has changed is the effectiveness of the human technology. But when that fails, the appeal to the supernatural is just as fervent and earnest as it has ever been.

Having considered what might be thought of as these two negative comparisons between the Middle Ages and contemporary Western religious identity, I now move on to the positive. In the next chapter I shall ask whether there are comparisons to be drawn between medieval religion and contemporary Western religious identity. Are there ways in which Christianity in the Middle Ages provides tools for understanding religion in the modern West?

Chapter Six

Contemporary and Medieval Christian Life

The focus of this chapter, as with the previous one, is the Christian life of ordinary people in the Middle Ages. In Chapter Five, I concentrated on what was different about the medieval period when compared with our own. I looked at churchgoing and argued that the extent to which it occurred in the Middle Ages would often depend on local factors. A conscientious priest working in a community with a local church might well encourage a good number to attend. An absentee priest who was ignorant and immoral would not attract many to Mass. I also looked at supernatural belief. I found that Christianity fulfilled a technological function for people which has now been taken over by science, especially medical science. So, whereas before people made pilgrimages to shrines to request cures or lit candles in storms to ward off demons, now they visit hospitals or doctors' surgeries and avoid standing under trees or near metal conductors.

In this chapter I will concentrate on the similarities between contemporary religious practice in secular society and what happened during the medieval period. When I say 'contemporary religious practice', I mean more than just modern churchgoers. What I have in mind is the 75 per cent or so of people who are generally supportive of Christianity and who express a belief in God. It is these people who make up secular society, so they are the important focus for comparison. What is interesting is the way in which medieval religious life and practice sheds light on modern-day Western society.

There are three areas I am going to explore in detail. The first is knowledge about the Christian faith amongst the majority of the population during the Middle Ages. I am not asking whether there was a lot of or a little Christian knowledge. It would in any case be difficult to calculate this given the amount of historical data that exists. Furthermore, there are complex problems such as the difference in levels of knowledge, especially between social classes. Rather, we discover that in the late Middle Ages people knew enough of what they needed to know to be able to interact with the Church in a way they found satisfactory. People in medieval society were equipped with what I shall describe as sufficient functional knowledge. By this I mean people had adequate understanding to allow religion to perform the role they required of it. This does not mean the Church was happy with the general level of Christian knowledge. The Church wanted people to know more. But most people were not concerned with the Church's priorities and concerns. The majority of the population knew what they needed to know so that Christianity could function in their interests. And the same is true of religious belief in the West today. A majority of people know what they need to know so that religion serves their particular ends.

I am then going to examine a concept suggested by Grace Davie in her analysis of contemporary Western religion. This is the notion that for many people their religion is vicarious. That is they like to know that other people are engaging in religious belief and practice on their behalf, but this does not necessarily mean they themselves will actively take part. If the religious activity is threatened or is perceived to be incorrectly undertaken, then people will complain. The threat to close a local church will often galvanize a community to campaign for the building to remain open. But they would not expect to become active members of the congregation. The willingness in the media to expose religious hypocrisy, for example when a cleric transgresses, is an illustration of the desire to ensure that those who practise religion do so with integrity. What is condemned amongst the clergy might nevertheless be more generously tolerated within wider society. The expectations of the religious practitioner are different because they are religious on behalf of the community.

This vicarious principle was also at work in medieval Christianity. For medieval people, the focus of vicarious religion was the saints. They were important because they intercede on behalf of ordinary Christians. What matters is not imitating the saints' behaviour and thereby living a good life, but winning the support of a saint to ensure protection and good fortune. In both contemporary and medieval times, a majority of people wish to see religious behaviour occurring, but they do not see it as their main role to maintain or propagate these activities.

The third area of comparison is ethics. Ethical considerations were central to medieval Christianity. Medieval people were concerned with those who were poorest and weakest in society. This found expression in the teachings concerning the 'Seven Works of Mercy' and in the poor dole handed out at funerals. This ethical priority continues to pervade twenty-first century ethics in the West. This is a controversial proposition and will need further elaboration in later chapters. The intention here is to lay down a marker for a topic I shall return to later.

It is as a result of making these comparisons that we gain more insight into the religious identity of Western secular society. What we shall find is that the contemporary West is informed, for its own purposes, about the Christian faith, concerned that those whose task it are able and willing to perform their religion well, and that it is guided by an ethical priority to the poorest and weakest.

The People's Theology

It is a common complaint amongst clergy that a majority of people are ignorant of the basics of the Christian faith. This applies in the West today and was equally applicable in the medieval period. Not enough is known about the Bible stories, or the history of the Church or basic doctrines. Sometimes implicit in this critique is the assumption that the Church would prosper if those ignorant of the faith knew what it was they were rejecting or ignoring.

This clerical concern about the extent of Christian knowledge amongst the population reveals an important distinction. It is a distinction between the popular faith of the majority of ordinary people and the work of official or designated academic and Church theologians. The distinction is made by Werner Ustorf, Professor of Mission at Birmingham University, in his chapter in the collection of essays published as *Dare We Speak of God in Public?*[1] Once we are clear about the nature of this distinction, we can then investigate what people knew about their faith during the Middle Ages.

On one side of the distinction is the official theology of the authorities. Christian theology as an academic and Church discipline seeks to speak coherently and critically about the Christian tradition, the Church's history and the continuing life of faith. This type of theological work has a limited but harmonious form which is controlled by intellectuals. There are conventions and rules which dictate how such theology is examined and presented. Those inducted into its ways are given time and space to explore in dialogue their ideas and experiences with others similarly inducted. This is not to denigrate the form or dismiss its value. The critical exploration of theological issues and themes by those well versed in its subtleties is extremely important. It has been a beneficial tool for advancing our understanding of God, the Church and its traditions. Without in-depth critical analysis, especially of religious beliefs, there is the danger we are left with nothing more than prejudice and perpetual ignorance.

Werner Ustorf is suspicious that such academic and Church theology is bound up with the power of Western society. It has a patriarchal, elitist and colonial history. In this he is influenced by theologies from the so-called Third World. These seek to reject First World theological techniques because they have not led to the liberation of poor and oppressed peoples. Third World theologies, and especially liberation theologies, begin with the experiences and struggles for justice of the poorest in the world. The questions, issues and topics of First World theologians have been able to avoid the perspectives of people outside of the inner circle. They are not concerned with the less systematic beliefs of non-academics. As such, Church and academic theologies relegate the popular religion of most people to a second-class status. This is because they do not make it the subject of their studies and their studies dominate theological work in universities.

We will see that academic and Church theology was highly influential during the medieval period. Church authorities believed that the lack of Christian knowledge, meaning knowledge of orthodox, official Church teaching, amongst the general population was a serious problem. There is plenty of evidence of both the local population and local clergy being judged ignorant of the essentials of the faith. However, alongside the condemnation of ignorance amongst the population, there are also signs that a functional popular religion operated just beyond the Church. This religion was the major priority of most people and they were skilled practitioners of it. Its majority status made it in many ways more important than the official teachings of the Church.

This takes us to the other side of the distinction, namely unofficial popular religion. What a majority of people have is an expertise in popular religion. Such popular religion is functional. It is employed by people to meet their daily concerns. Ustorf describes it thus:

> The religions of so-called ordinary people consist
> usually of the simple expectations in relation to life:

that one has to eat, that the crop is good or employment
continues, that the child regains health, that debt will
not become intolerable and war does not threaten, that
one has people to talk to, that one stays alive and will
die peacefully, having a decent burial. The people's
religious discourse is often very careful not to go beyond
one's own authority: they do not try to 'explain' or to
'know' or even to define God.[2]

The aims of popular religion are not academically rigorous;
there is no attempt at coherence or systematics, but they are
vastly more ambitious. Popular religion aims to provide the
resources by which a person can lead a safe and contented life.
More is demanded of popular religion than the truth about
God. It is asked to shape the experience of the individual and
community so that happiness is achieved. Besides such enormous demands, the expectations attached to official Church
and academic theology seem rather insignificant.

When we consider the evidence from the medieval period,
we see both forms of popular religion and also official Church
and academic theology. The interrogation of a Spanish peasant
in 1518 is an excellent example of this dual religious identity
at work. At one level it is illustrative of the ignorance of the
peasantry. At another level, however, the interrogation demonstrates how popular religion functioned. The peasant, who is
being questioned about visions he had experienced, is a prisoner of the Holy Office of the Inquisition. The report of the
questioning is as follows:

> He was asked by his Reverence if he knew the Credo
> and Salve Regina: he said he did not. Asked if he knew
> the Pater Nostra and Ave Maria; he said he did. He was
> ordered to say them. He said the entire Ave Maria, and
> the Pater Nostra he said in its entirety but he did not
> know it well. He was asked by his Reverence if he
> confessed every year as Holy Mother Church mandates.
> He said that he has confessed every year at Lent with

the old priest in the town of La Mota, and that every time he confessed he received the most holy sacrament.

Asked if he knew the Ten Commandments and the Articles of Faith and the seven deadly sins and the five senses, he said he did not know any of these in whole or in part. Asked by his reverence what he confessed, if he did not know the seven deadly sins or the Ten Commandments or the five senses, he said he confessed what he did know about. He was asked if pride or envy or lust or the killing of a man or insulting someone with offensive words was a sin, and to each of these he replied he did not know. He was asked if theft was a sin, and he said that, God preserve us, theft was a very great sin.[3]

The contrast between what the Church authorities considered the basics of the Christian faith and the faith of the peasant is clear. For the authorities, personal confession without a basic knowledge of what constitutes sin is an impossibility. For the peasant, the sin that appears to have mattered was theft. It is only speculation, but one assumes that the other listed sins, pride, envy, lust and murder, were either entirely beyond the experience of the peasant or so much a part of life that it was not conceivable for him to think of them as sin.

There are two sets of conclusions that can be drawn from this illustration. It could be taken to show the high levels of ignorance about the Christian faith amongst poor people. This would be a reasonable conclusion reached by official Church and theological authorities. The emergence after the thirteenth century of teaching material for poorly educated clergy, so that they could educate their congregations in the basics of the faith, are illustrative both of the attempts of Church leaders to address the problem of general ignorance and also of the actual problem itself. If there was a good knowledge of basic Christianity then such books would not be required. Duffy argues that the requirement of annual confession, imposed by the Fourth Lateran Council in 1215, provided local clergy with an educational as well as pastoral tool. Much of the teaching literature arose to meet this need. It was recognized that a lot of clergy could not undertake the task unassisted.

However, this is only the first conclusion to be drawn. In amongst the peasant's failed answers and stuttering attempt to recite the Lord's Prayer, there is a confident statement that theft was a sin. There is also the knowledge that he must confess once a year and receive communion. If we apply Ustorf's distinction here, it might be argued that what the example illustrates is religions in parallel. The peasant does not know Church theology. But he does have a strong sense of right and wrong when it comes to theft. He also knows to confess once a year and receive communion. In other words, there is something popular and unofficial happening here which manages simultaneously to slip beneath the radar of Church and academic theology and yet occasionally interact with it.

There are plenty more examples of this functional popular religion at work in medieval society. In fact, the conditions of the Middle Ages bring it to the fore. For example, prior to the establishment of the parish system and the advent of local clergy with responsibility for teaching, the basics of the Christian faith was transmitted informally. Families would be responsible for communicating Christianity to their children. What was transmitted was not academic. Those with even partial knowledge of the Bible were extremely rare. Towards the end of the Middle Ages, and with the arrival of printing, still the majority of people did not know the Bible beyond a few key texts. But, and this is the point of the distinction between popular religion and official theology, they did not need such knowledge. What people required was a sound understanding of how to maintain a happy life. What they needed was to be effective participants in public ceremonies and knowledgeable practitioners of the ways of garnishing the benefits available from God. For the latter, as we have seen and will discuss more below, the favour of saints was key. For the former it was a matter of sharing in the rites of the local church and the social activities of the local community. For most medieval people, important knowledge was knowledge of how to be skilled players in the local festivals, including understanding their significance in daily life.

There were a good number of such festival celebrations. Candlemas, celebrated 40 days after Christmas, was an important festival in the Church's year. Candles would be blessed prior to the Mass.[4] The blessed candles would then be taken home to be lit during thunderstorms to ward off demons or to be placed in the hands of the sick and dying. Another important celebration was for the feast of Corpus Christi. By the end of the Middle Ages this would involve large processions through the local town or village. The procession reflected the social order of precedence in the community. Local guilds, the means by which many people could afford to pay for religious practices, became the key organizing body for these elaborate processions. Duffy argues that most lay people were heavily caught up in the Holy Week ceremonials. There would be services to mark Palm Sunday, Maundy Thursday, Good Friday, Holy Saturday and of course Easter Sunday itself. During Holy Week, people would find a priest to hear their confession so that they could receive communion on Easter Day. There are stories of extra priests being required because of the high demand for confessions. The problem of absentee priests was that they were not available for confession at Easter or for that matter for the death bed confessions and last rites. Christmas was also an important time. And alongside the major festivals would be a number of celebrations for particular saints such as Mary, St Thomas Becket, St Anne, St George and many others.

Duffy believes these services and ceremonies were a vehicle for teaching the Church's basic doctrine, the important elements of the doctrine of salvation being taught during Holy Week for example. This is probably true for the devout and enthusiastic. However, alongside the real devotion of some, for many the festivals were a chance to escape the daily grind and participate in the rites of popular religion. It was a day off work and the chance to enjoy to the full community celebrations. I have already noted how much ale was drunk normally and we can assume people did not hold back when they were celebrating. Sometimes local gentry were required to provide refreshments. It would have been an occasion for social interaction. But more important than either of these aspects, we can also speculate that for a majority of people the religious ceremonies would have had a significance they understood but which was not part of the official Church's teaching. People shared in the Church's liturgy as an expression of their own popular devotion. This devotion was functional. The participation in religious practice expressed a religious belief system which tied together some elements of basic theology with the desire for happiness and security. And what they needed to know was what to participate in, and when and how to do it. So one received communion at Easter after confession, one collected a blessed candle at Candlemas and one processed at Corpus Christi. In this way, one did what was reasonable and proper and right. Religion, and especially the basics of religious faith, are thereby negotiated effectively.

Something very similar occurs in the West today. There are mass communal celebrations which have a religious underpinning, but which do not conform precisely to the Church's official teaching. The majority of people know enough to know what to take from the Church and how to use it, without needing to explore theology or doctrine in any great depth. The celebration of Christmas is an example of this and not just the Church's services at and around Christmas Day, but the multitude of carol services and parties which surround the festival. The clergy often have a major role at this time. This role is ambiguous. Part of it is spent trying to teach the 'real' meaning of Christmas. But another part is spent conforming to the popular notion of what Christmas should be as taught by society. Clergy are highly unpopular if they challenge the popular knowledge of what Christmas is and means. To a lesser extent the same could be said about Easter. This strong local knowledge of what the Christian faith should be and how it functions also applies to baptisms and funerals. People come to these important rituals knowing what to expect of each participant in the drama. A popular knowledge underpins the rituals without the need for explicit teaching.[5]

This brings us back to the question of knowledge and ignorance of the Christian faith. In one sense the majority of people are ignorant of the basics of Christianity. This would be the Church and academic theological perspective. However, at another level the majority of people know enough about how their faith and beliefs function to meet their own requirements. They interact with the Church for the fulfilment of the popular religion they understand superbly. What this means is that large parts of society were superstitious in the Middle Ages, or secular in the contemporary period, because ignorance prevailed. But it can also be said that at the same time the majority of the population were skilled practitioners of a popular religion which served their needs. In fact, of the contemporary West, we can say that one characteristic of secular society is the excellent knowledge people have of how popular religion should function.

Vicarious Religion

In her book *Religion in Modern Europe*, Grace Davie argues that the boundary around Church identity is blurred. Some people, in all likelihood a large number, interact with the Church vicariously. That is, they look to the Church to 'perform a number of tasks on behalf of the population as a whole'.[6] Davie has in mind both family services such as baptisms, wedding and funerals, and also the national or state occasions when a society comes together to mourn or celebrate. Vicarious Church supporters require the Church to be alive and ongoing, but do not consider it their responsibility to participate in its regular life. If the Church was not available or was not willing to undertake certain liturgical tasks, despite their lack of regular involvement, then they would be deeply shocked. We can speculate that the 75 per cent or so whom we have identified as being supportive but not regularly involved in Church life share this perspective. They will look to the Church in times of crisis and expect it to be ready for them at such times, but this does not translate into an activist religious commitment.

This vicarious attitude to religion is sometimes attributed to the consumerist mentality characteristic of contemporary Western citizens. What is expected from the Church is a service in the sense that the same would be expected from a health provider, local garage or department store. However, this is not the argument here. The idea of vicarious religion has a much longer history. We can see evidence of the vicarious principle at work in medieval Christianity. It may well be that vicarious religion is a stable characteristic of religious belief and behaviour throughout different historical eras and cultures. To understand how vicarious religion was at work during the Middle Ages, we need to grasp something of what constituted broader Christian practice. In particular, we need to understand the role played by the veneration of saints.

Medieval people did not believe they could reach heaven by their own efforts. They lacked the moral skill necessary to achieve salvation. They therefore depended on the intercessions of saints. The goodness and holiness of saints provided a spiritual trump card in the efforts to win God's mercy. The saint's good standing allowed them access to God so that they could plead for mercy on behalf of their clients. Saints were the patrons of flawed humanity in the court of the divine. If suitable representations were made, an individual or community had a powerful friend who might negotiate favours from God. What this meant was that the primary role of the saint was not as a model for imitation. There was no expectation that ordinary people would themselves behave like saints. Rather, they depended on the intercessions of the saints for their spiritual well-being. The saint was to be courted rather than copied. The example of virginity illustrates this point.

Virginity has had a high prestige value in Christian history since the teachings of St Paul. However, most men and women did not expect to remain virgins throughout their lives. They expected to raise families and take partners in the time-honoured fashion. But medieval people valued the power that was associated with virginity. Duffy argues that what virginity offered most people was 'not so much a model to imitate, something most of them never dreamt of doing, but rather a source of power to be tapped'. The popularity of many women saints was due to the value placed on their heroic defence of their virginity. In fact, the virgin saint could well be appealed to for a fruitful marriage bed and as protection against miscarriage. And whilst virginity was the special case, the principle applied to all saints. They were powerful friends in times of immediate need, including at the point of death and afterwards.

The extension of this principle led to the offering of indulgences. The rewards of the saints' excess holiness could be shared amongst the generally sinful population. Indulgences could be earned by making pilgrimages to shrines, by saying prayers at the elevation of the Host, and eventually by simple purchase. The extent to which this was or was not a corrupt system does not concern us here. Rather, indulgences enshrined the principle of vicarious religion. What mattered was not the individual's own especial holiness, but their capacity to draw upon the spiritual capital generated by the holiness of others. The principle is further illustrated by the idea of pilgrimage by proxy. The request that pilgrimages be taken by others on the individual's behalf was merely an extension of the idea of vicarious religion. Ronald Finucane argues that 'pilgrimages by proxy' were common and a feature of many wills. People with sufficient resources were keen that the promises they had made during life, and for which they would now have to give account, were undertaken at their expense if not actually by them in person.[7]

It should be clear that when we discuss vicarious religion we are not arguing that the individual has no role in religious practice. In medieval society, as in contemporary society, the individual has an important part to play. It is their responsibility to ensure that they take advantage of the merits won and offered by others. What the vicarious principle does is delineate the various roles of different parties. A minority will be religious activists pursuing a life of personal holiness. In the medieval period the pinnacle of achievement was saintliness. In our own times in the West the role of excellent religious practitioner has been adopted by the abstract notion of Church. Individuals associated with Church may not actually be required to be saints, but they are required to conform to certain standards and offer service at moments of high social drama. Then for the majority the aim is to be associated with this minority at certain crucial moments. For medieval people the moment par excellence was the time of death and the last spiritual struggles of life. For the contemporary West such moments come as a result of exceptional cultural events, such as the death of Princess Diana, and when families require the Church to endorse their rites of passage. At these moments what is required is a Church which is spiritually equipped to perform its role to the satisfaction of earth and, less concretely, heaven.

For the modern Church to be able to fulfil its side of the bargain, it has to be very cautious about the introduction of new ideas. One suspects that, when the Church seeks to adapt to changing social mores such as the controversy about the ordination of gay and lesbian people, one implicit element of the debate for many people is whether the Church's holiness will be undermined by such a change. The question is whether a Church with people of diverse sexualities, whatever the theological rights and wrongs, can still effectively intercede with the Divine. Is it still holy enough? Of course it is, but the need is for concrete proof that the Church's communication with the Divine still works properly. Likewise, a bishop who seeks to speak about some of the theological issues which impact on official Church discourses can find his reasonable questioning subject to the irrational fear that a sacred role has been jeopardized. Again, what this means for the secular identity of Western society is important. One aspect of Western secularism is the expectation that some people, the

Church, will practise religion on behalf of a majority. This majority will turn to the Church at crucial moments of their lives and inspect its activities, but will not feel an ongoing responsibility for its existence. For most people a characteristic of secular society is that it has a functioning Church ensuring links with the Divine, so that these are available to people in times of need.

Caring for the Poor and Weak

The third and final area for comparison is the area of ethics. There is a danger that medieval society is too frequently portrayed as self-interested. In particular, people in the Middle Ages can seem excessively concerned with what might happen to them after death. It is true that medieval society lived with a real fear of the afterlife and its expected punishments. The tortures the damned soul might anticipate were frequently described in graphic and vivid detail. Every type of physical punishment imaginable was a likely consequence of earthly transgression. Often the punishment was made to fit the crime. So those who had committed sexual crimes were tortured in their loins, the gluttonous were force fed revolting substances and those who lied would have their tongues sliced up.[8] The fear of such torture led to a major effort on the part of most people to win the support of saints at the moment of judgment. It also led to the widespread request for prayers for souls of the departed. Intercessions were offered for the dead so that their pains may be eased and shortened. One feature of wills was the distribution of funds for such prayers.

However, it would be a mistake to see medieval Christianity as a purely self-interested religion. There was more to it than efforts directed towards the alleviation of the punishments of purgatory. Medieval Christianity also had a strong ethical element. This was caught up in the concerns about moral failure and its consequences after death, but it was not dominated by such concerns. Furthermore, this ethical code had a distinct form. It is one so familiar to us in the West that we tend to take it for granted. It was a concern for those who were poorest and most vulnerable. Such a care for the weakest is by no means obvious in all societies and cultures throughout human history.

The evidence for the existence and importance of this ethical code is strong. In particular, amidst the teachings and devotional practices of the medieval Church were the Seven Works of Mercy. These were:

> You shall feed the hungry, give drink to the thirsty, visit those who are sick, harbor those that have need, clothe the naked, comfort those in prison, bury Christian bodies that are dead: these are the VII Works of Mercy.[9]

These teachings have a clear origin in the parable of the goats and sheep in chapter 25 of Matthew's Gospel. It would be easy to see that these are merely pious platitudes which, alongside the functional religion we have so far described, had no real impact on people's behaviour. However, the parable was central to the eschatology of medieval society.[10] People will be judged not by the piety they profess or the doctrinal orthodoxy they claim, but by their actions towards those who were poor and weak. It was a clear expectation that a Christian soul would give alms to the poor. Interestingly, and slightly oddly for us today, what mattered was the gift itself more than the intention of the giver. The story circulated in medieval piety of a rich man who, for want of a better missile, throws a hard loaf at a poor man. At the moment of judgment the rich man is won from the devil by the Virgin, who cites this hostile act as an incidence of charity, albeit of a singularly begrudging kind.

An important moment to demonstrate charitable concern to those in need was the funeral dole. The funeral was the last moment at which alms might be distributed to the poor. Hence in the provision of wills, of those who could afford it, money was set aside to give to the poor. Food, drink and clothing were handed out, or the funds for such provisions, by the executors of the will. This usually went with the request for prayers on behalf of the deceased person. Even when explicit bequests were not made, it was such a feature of the funeral ceremonies that some provision was made anyway. Often the alms would be bestowed on the poor of the deceased's parish. The funeral dole may or may not have been a sign of previous generosity to the poor. For the deceased, the moment of individual judgment was very immediate. The value of the funeral dole was that it highlighted the poor aided by the wealthy individual at the very moment of judgment. This was deemed strong evidence of personal charity. As the practice developed, it became common for poor people to be gathered around the coffin as highly visible evidence that the dead soul deserved the mercy that he or she had shown on earth.

The Works of Mercy were not the only ethical criteria by which the dead soul was judged. The seven mortal sins were also a feature of the annual confession prior to Easter communion. But the concern for the poor and weak had an especial significance. More than this, it remains a characteristic of the ethics of Western society. Even without the threats of purgatory or hell, there is still a requirement on Western society to care for the less fortunate. It is difficult to imagine an ethical system which neglects the poorest or which prioritizes the wealthiest. The resilience of the Welfare State in the UK is evidence of this ethical concern. The Welfare State is a structural social expression of a priority that the poorest be clothed, fed, housed, care for and educated. In principle this is the case, however imperfect the practice might be. When the social consensus around welfare provision is under attack, as during the early part of the Thatcher government, even so the moral principle is protected. In a nation such as the USA, which can appear to depend upon a cultural ethics of self-achievement and when welfare provision is weak, even so the moral code that underpins society allows for the success of the poorest. The principle is that first some provision is in place for those who fail to live the American dream, whilst the dream itself only makes ethical sense if it is available to all. Again the practice undoubtedly falls short, but the ethical case depends on the poorest having opportunity. I shall explore this point in more detail in the final chapter of the book. Our work on the Enlightenment is crucial for this case. At this stage, the point is that there is a close affinity between Western contemporary and medieval ethics. The same principle of concern for the poor and weakest underpins both societies. So we can hazard, with a recognition of the need for more explanation later, that a further feature of Western secular society is an ethics grounded within and dependent upon medieval Christianity. In other words, the ethics of secularism is in essence Christian.

The comparisons I have drawn show that there are common features to both contemporary Western religious identity and medieval Christianity. Both societies are characterized by a technical knowledge of popular religion. This knowledge is shared by a majority of the population. It differs from the official orthodoxy of the Church and academic theological establishment. The establishment will often miss its value and importance, but it is a powerful resource for people as they seek contentment and security. Alongside popular religion there is also the notion of vicarious religion at work. A majority of people expect others to be performing a religious function on their behalf. They do not expect to carry out this religious practice themselves, but they monitor its performance so that they can be sure it will be available to them when they need it. Western secular society is both technically proficient at religion and skilled at evaluating the implications of any religious change amidst the bodies it expects to carry out religion normally. Finally, we have noted the ethical underpinning of medieval society: there is a concern for the poorest and weakest. This ethical concern remains after a lot of the public practice of religion has diminished, such as in Western society. The ethics of Western society only make sense in light of this Christian heritage. This point will become clearer as we progress through the next chapter. This is concerned with the events of the Enlightenment. It is at the Enlightenment that we see a change in public discussions. What is important is that an ethics founded in Christianity survives the attacks made on the Church.

Chapter Seven

The Enlightenment Effect

The Enlightenment was a major event in Western history. Its impact has been experienced in almost all areas of human endeavour from the mid-late seventeenth century up to and including our own times. It is only from the second half of the twentieth century that we have begun to think in terms of a post-Enlightenment or post-modern era, and this is a much disputed topic. In this chapter, I shall focus on two areas of the Enlightenment which are especially relevant to my investigations. The first is the development of a scientific mentality. I initially discussed this in Chapter Two. Those who argue that secularism is a result of progress in human thought cite the scientific mentality as a key example of increased human sophistication. This mentality arose during the Enlightenment period. In this chapter, I shall analyse its development in more detail.

The second area of investigation is the ongoing Christian identity of contemporary Western liberal ethics. There are certain principles and values which are common in secular society and have their roots in Christian theology. The ongoing importance of these principles and values demonstrates the extent to which Christianity, or at the very least a

Christian heritage, is significant for any understanding of Western secular society. In this chapter, I shall explore what these principles and values are and how they relate to Christian theology.

The aim of this chapter is to argue that Western secular society is characterized by a dual identity. A scientific mentality, which replaced Christianity as the West's dominant technology, coexists with a Christian ethics supported by a resilient popular belief in God. In one sense, I am suggesting that Steve Bruce is correct when he says that what people mean when they say they believe in God is that they are good, decent people. But this is not because I think the statement of belief is vacuous and devoid of theological meaning. It is because I am speculating that people are concerned about ethics, about how to be good, and they believe that a notion of God is important in their efforts. They employ belief in God as part of their ethical endeavour. This is the role Christianity continues to play in Western society. An identifiably Christian ethics, underpinned by belief in God, is the guide to the way in which most people wish to behave when they wish to behave well.

The chapter begins with the question of what is the Enlightenment. This will identify the period I am calling the Enlightenment and describe the key ideas which characterized the age. This is as much a description of an ethos and atmosphere as it is any new scientific discoveries or philosophical systems. I shall then examine the development of the scientific mentality. This will include a discussion of the importance of Sir Isaac Newton. The third section looks at the relationship between the Enlightenment and Christianity. I will examine two aspects of this relationship. First, I shall explore the nature and extent of the anti-Christian sentiment. The Enlightenment is known as a time when some launched scathing attacks on the Church and Christian belief. Second, I investigate the Christian identity of Western liberal ethics. What is it that makes liberalism in its current Western form Christian? This discussion is of fundamental importance to the case I am making in this book.

What I am proposing is that Western secular society is scientific in its technology and Christian in its ethics.

What is the Enlightenment?

The question 'What is enlightenment?' has occupied some of the greatest minds in human history. Included in this list is the most important philosopher of the Enlightenment and, some would argue, the Modern era, Immanuel Kant. The question is different from the one which asks 'What is the Enlightenment?'. The former asks about the intellectual ideas and cultural ethos which make up the phenomenon known as enlightenment. The latter is more prosaic in that it asks which historical period is being discussed and who were the key thinkers and writers. But the two questions are inter-related. The thinkers and writers who created the new ethos had the original ideas which made the historical period so distinctive. I shall therefore look at both questions. I begin by identifying the historical period under discussion before moving on to investigate the ethos of enlightenment.

Professor Peter Gay, in his magisterial two-volume history, identifies the eighteenth century as the key period of the Enlightenment.[1] He suggests two evocative dates as convenient boundaries. The beginning can be dated from 1688 and the Glorious Revolution in England; the end can be marked by the French Revolution of 1789. This is not to suggest that Enlightenment ideas were unknown before 1688. Nor did the ideas disappear after the great upheaval of the French Revolution, far from it. But before the eighteenth century the ideas lacked the revolutionary force which was to make them so important for the Modern period. And after 1789 the atmosphere and ethos changed. Whilst the Enlightenment continued to be influential for generations to come, nevertheless the intellectual and cultural climate which gave it its initial impetus came to an end.

Gay identifies three generations of writers within the period.[2] These men (they were all men) were the key figures

who set the tone of the Enlightenment. It is useful to list them
so that we know whom I am discussing when I talk about the
Enlightenment. The first generation was dominated by
Montesquieu and Voltaire. They drew on the work of John
Locke and Isaac Newton whilst it was still new and challeng-
ing. The second generation was born near the beginning of the
century and grew to maturity during its mid-point. It
included Franklin, Hume, Rousseau, Diderot and his co-
worker on the famous *Encyclopédie*, d'Alembert. It was this generation which created the new and original modern worldview.
The third generation included Holbach, Lessing, Jefferson,
Kant and Turgot. These writers and thinkers drew upon and
developed the work of earlier 'philosophes', taking the
Enlightenment in new directions in the fields of philosophy,
science, economics, law and politics.[3] As we shall see below,
Gay's list is by no means uncontroversial.

It is clear that each of these generations is interrelated.
Voltaire did an enormous amount to popularize Newton's scientific methodology and his discoveries. This was no mean
feat. Kant regarded Rousseau as one of his most important
influences and had a portrait of him in his study. Holbach
employed Hume in his anti-Christian attacks. The inter-
relation between these thinkers was in part evolutionary.
Later generations of writers could build on the work of their
forerunners. It was also, according to Gay, illustrative of the
consensus that existed through the Enlightenment period. It
demonstrated the important coherence which was manifested
in the spirit of the age. The notion that there was a significant
coherence running through the Enlightenment has been heavily criticized in recent scholarship. Before we look at these
criticisms, we need first to understand the consensus which
Gay thought characterized the period.

Immanuel Kant answered the question 'What is enlightenment?' in an essay of that title, submitted in 1784 to the
Enlightenment journal *Berlinische Monatsschrift*.[4] This was his
entry into a competition organized by the publication. His first
paragraph is a famous summary of the Enlightenment ethos:

Enlightenment is man's release from his self-incurred tutelage. Tutelage is man's inability to make use of his understanding without direction from another. Self-incurred is this tutelage when its cause lies not in lack of reason but in lack of resolution and courage to use it without direction from another. *Sapere aude!* [Dare to know!] 'Have courage to use your own reason!' – that is the motto of enlightenment.[5]

This quotation captures the sense of confidence and free-dom which pervaded the Enlightenment. The confidence came from the ability of humanity to fight back against nature. For centuries, if not for all of previous human history, people had been victims of nature. They had endured plagues and famines, floods and earthquakes, disease and starvation. Hanging over the head of humanity was the very real and oppressive sense that natural disaster awaited around the cor-ner. Alongside nature's cruelties were the wounds inflicted by humanity on itself. War and violence alternated with a fragile and uneasy peace. With the Enlightenment, all this began to change. Not overnight of course, it took time; but a new spirit emerged. Critical investigation, inquiry and, especially, the giant steps forward in science, meant human beings could begin to exercise power. They could learn to understand and control some of the forces arrayed against them. Life was no longer a series of unexplained and mysterious disasters. Knowledge and understanding, inquiry and criticism gave people a sense of freedom related to their exercise of power. And of these it was the critical spirit, the daring to know, to investigate, judge, analyse and understand that stood out as the tool for humanity's growth and success.

The Enlightenment period has sometimes been called the 'Age of Reason'. Peter Gay develops this idea. For him the Enlightenment is better described as the 'Age of Criticism'. The philosophes believed that reason was not the only tool of enlightenment. It did not necessarily lead to action, nor was it the sole instrument of effect inquiry.[6] The more encompassing idea of criticism fulfilled these roles. For criticism to occur, there needed to be two conditions in place. First, there had to be a sense of freedom. This was freedom from domineering institutions and ideas. It was a freedom to experiment, to learn new things and express new ideas. Second, there had to be people or structures to criticize. There needed to be objects of criticism. The eighteenth century provided two of these: the Church and the political establishment. They were the targets of much often severe critical comment from the philosophes. In fact, what characterized the Enlightenment was the desire and willingness to criticize both religion and politics. This was not without its risks. The philosophes could fall foul of the authorities and suffer persecution. They sometimes needed to flee their homes for safe havens in more liberal countries. But they persevered with their criticisms of Church and state, and often doubled their efforts.

The inspiration for the philosophes' criticism came from Greek and Roman classical sources. Peter Gay described the philosophes as 'modern pagans'. What the philosophes did was utilize their classical learning as a tool for criticizing Christianity. The ancients were a means of liberating them from their Christian heritage and tutelage. Then, having dispensed with the services of the classics, they turned and constructed a modern worldview. The Enlightenment was 'a volatile mixture of classicism, impiety, and science', and it was this that made them modern pagans.[7] The modern worldview these men sought was then ably summarized:

> The men of the Enlightenment united on a vastly
> ambitious program, a program of secularism, humanity,
> cosmopolitanism, and freedom, above all, freedom in
> its many forms – freedom from arbitrary power, freedom
> of speech, freedom of trade, freedom to realize one's
> talents, freedom of aesthetic response, freedom, in a
> word, of moral man to make his own way in the
> world.[8]

Humanity had grown up. People were now adults, able to make their own way in the world. They did not need the myths and superstitions of the Church to comfort them and explain their lives. Nor did they need the guardianship of oppressive political regimes. People could and should embrace their new freedom and knowledge. In the spirit of the age, humanity was primed for a glorious future as it grew in understanding and ability. With science positioned at the vanguard and religion confined to the dustbin of history, humanity was marching forward to a wonderful future. This was enlightenment.

Or, at least, this was the vision of enlightenment. Clearly no one believed all the possibilities could be fulfilled immediately. In Kant's well-known phrase not everyone was enlightened, but it was the Age of Enlightenment. What we have described is the spirit of the new age. There was an enlightenment temper which was hopeful and confident. This said we should not present this vision without discussing some major qualifications. The first is less serious. It is presented by Gay in his study.[9] This was the recognition that there were important national variations in the development of the Enlightenment. For example, the French, in their lead up to revolution, were highly critical of both Church and State. In comparison, the English were generally content with their religious and political institutions, they had had their revolution, and the Germans were 'almost wholly unpolitical'. Gay stated that the Italians tended to work with the state to bring about change. So in very general terms, Gay was aware that there were differences of culture and history which impacted on the main priorities of the philosophes. But these differences did not amount to sufficient variation to challenge the unity of the Enlightenment. There was a consensus in spirit and a shared identity. In fact, there was enough common cause that the philosophes should be thought of as one family, albeit a frequently argumentative family. The Enlightenment ethos was so dominant that these regional differences did not undo the shared spirit of the age.

However, others have not been so convinced about the unity of what I am calling the Enlightenment. In particular, it is argued that our picture of the Enlightenment is male and elitist. It is concerned with great men and their thoughts.[10] What is missing are the contributions of women, of the poor and oppressed, and of non-Western voices. For example, the majority of literature written during the Enlightenment period was not engaged in discussing big ideas about science and philosophy. This literature consisted of travel guides, popular novels, pornography, children's books and textbooks on classical history. The great majority of these books have drifted into obscurity, but their production constituted the main economics of the Enlightenment. Michel Foucault has described the fate of the social outcast during the Enlightenment. A consequence of defining reason and reasonableness was the institutionalization of people whom society had previously accommodated in less inhumane ways. In Gay's study some women are acknowledged as having a role, but this is frequently as confidante and lover. Their contribution to ideas has often been glossed over by scholars. Finally, what enlightenment meant to many people in Western colonies was far different from the experience of the favoured few in Western Europe. Scientific technology has had many appalling consequences in warfare and genocide, as well as undoubted medical benefits. So our unified picture of the Enlightenment as a time of scientific and intellectual advance has missed out many significant people. This is after all human history and as such it is rarely, if ever, straightforward.

The question is whether these different histories make any attempt to summarize and define the Enlightenment a meaningless exercise. In one sense it does. We cannot hope to pay heed to all the different aspects of what was happening during the turbulent eighteenth century. But then to attempt a comprehensive history is not our aim. For the purposes of our investigations we do not need to analyse the role of the poor in revolutionary France. What I am concerned with is the shift in ideas around the subjects of science and ethics. For these issues it is sufficient to focus on the change in intellectual culture which was engineered by the philosophes whilst acknowledging that this is not the whole picture. Nor do I say that these changes were unequivocally good for all people. They clearly were not. But my focus is, at this stage, on the nature of the changes. It is in the final chapter that I consider some of the ethical questions which impact on our post-Enlightenment society. It is with this priority in mind that I move on to consider the development of a scientific mentality.

The Scientific Mentality

There are two outstanding achievements of the Enlightenment period. The first of these is the life and career of Sir Isaac Newton. The second is the production by Diderot, assisted in the early days by d'Alembert, of the *Encyclopédie*. What this remarkable life and vast undertaking illustrates is the new scientific mentality which was celebrated by the philosophes. In these two exemplars of enlightenment, old superstitions and myths were swept away by observation, detailed study and analysis. They are the crowning achievements of the age.

The eighteenth century was a time of incredible innovation and advance.[11] Samuel Johnson commented that 'the age is running mad after innovation; all the business of the world is to be done in a new way; men are to be hanged in a new way; Tyburn itself is not safe from the fury of innovation'.[12] It is a mute point whether the condemned convicts appreciated their participation in the age of advance. What is certain is that they were part of a wider experience of the novel and improved. The reason such innovation and change was so prevalent and triumphant is that it was deliberate and organized. Peter Gay describes the situation superbly:

> Scientific academies, established in the seventeenth century to facilitate the exchange and propagation of reliable technical information, served as a model for the eighteenth century. The age of the Enlightenment was an age of academies – academies of medicine, of

agriculture, of literature, each with its prizes, its journals, and its well-attended meetings. In the academies and outside them, in factories and workshops and coffeehouses, intelligence, liberated from the bonds of tradition, often heedless of aesthetic scruples or religious restraints, devoted itself to practical results; it kept in touch with scientists and contributed to technological refinements.[13]

The number of new discoveries, illustrated by patents granted, rose from on average 60 per decade between 1660 and 1760 to 325 between 1760 and 1790. This added to the sense that life was rapidly improving; by no means perfect of course, but distinctly better.

The most significant area of improvement was in medicine. Medicine was establishing itself on a firm scientific base. It was separating from the mysteries of alchemy and astrology and from the earlier randomness of family cures and intercession to the saints. It was absorbing the Enlightenment ethos of empirical study. Medical practitioners were often philosophers and many of the Enlightenment philosophes had studied medicine or were great friends with doctors. Medicine was the area in which the ideas of the Enlightenment brought greatest benefit to human welfare. People were no longer entirely victims of their bodily constitution. This is not to say the process of medical advance was not slow and resisted. Many quacks preyed on the innocent and ignorant. Professional medical bodies could be dominated by elderly practitioners sceptical of the benefits of the new science. The best in medical science was still beyond the finances of many. But the future of medicine was underpinned by the ethos of Enlightenment. The integration of medicine, philosophy and the spirit of the Enlightenment age is illustrated by one of the most famous physicians of the period, Hermann Boerhaave. His medical school at Leyden attracted students from all over Western Europe and the USA. What is interesting about his methodology is that he claimed it as Newtonian. This was the highest accolade of the Enlightenment. It was a sign that the old methods of superstition and metaphysical 'hypotheses' had been abandoned in favour of the new and innovative. Boerhaave's claim to be Newtonian leads us to examine the importance of the great man.

Sir Isaac Newton stands out as the great hero of the Enlightenment. He is acknowledged as the man who laid many of the foundations of modern science. Born in 1642, he became Lucasian Professor of Mathematics at Cambridge in 1669, having, at the age of 23, worked out the fundamentals of calculus. His greatest work was the *Mathematical Principles of Natural Philosophy*, published in Latin in 1687, revised in 1713 and then 1726, and published in English in 1729.[14] His work was popularized by Voltaire, who called him the greatest man that ever lived. Voltaire wrote that:

> If true greatness consists of having been endowed
> by heavens with powerful genius, and of using it to
> enlighten oneself and others, then a man like
> M. Newton (we scarcely find one like him in ten
> centuries) is truly great, and those politicians and
> conquerors (whom no century has been without) are
> generally nothing but celebrated villains.[15]

Voltaire was never afraid of hyperbole. But his description and the work he did to promote Newton are fitting testimonies to the fundamental importance of Newton. Newton's influence was universal. His scientific methodology, the employment of mathematics, observation and experiment, was imitated in all of the developing fields of natural and social science. Voltaire stated that 'we are all his disciples now'. Hume sought to become the 'Newton of the moral sciences'.[16] And Newton conformed to the picture of enlightenment genius. He was eccentric, absorbed by his study and above the polemics which surrounded his discoveries. He was a visionary who revealed the mysteries of the universe. The stories about him, not least of which is the falling apple, added to the aura of genius. Furthermore, regardless of the actual standing of his scientific work, he embodied for us and for the philosophes the essence of the intellectual revolution that occurred at the Enlightenment.

Newton's achievement, especially in France, was to overturn the dominance of Descartes' methodology. I do not need to examine this in detail. Suffice it to say that, whereas Descartes employed a deductive reasoning to explain natural phenomena, Newton was empirical and inductive. Descartes would not use the senses to investigate the universe. He employed rational thinking to explore the world around him. Newton investigated the detail. His theories were built on his observations and analysis. This led Newton, particularly in the second book of his masterpiece, to expose some of the absurdities of Descartes' cosmology. Newton could reduce Descartes' notion that the universe was full of matter or that the planets were dragged around the sun in vortices to nonsense through his rigorous empirical investigations. Newton's science was by far the more successful. After Newton, it was apparent to all interested in the subject that a better explanation of the universe came through the laws of gravitation. These victories in physics and astronomy led to the dominance of the Newtonian way in all aspects of science, including the medical and social sciences. The positing of hypotheses based on deductive reasoning had no place in a world of empirical science, of experiment and observation.

This is the triumph of the scientific mentality. It is not the unquestioning adoption of Newtonian physics in all its details; even Newton has not fully stood the test of time. But it is the triumph at a popular level of empiricism over metaphysics. The public sphere requires facts and explanations which depend on observation and inductive reasoning. This is true in the social sciences as much as the natural sciences. It is the mentality which dominates secular Western society and with which religion has struggled to coexist. It remains despite the questioning of post-modernity, as I shall argue in the final chapter.

This brings me to the last point to be made about Newton.[17] He remained throughout his life a Christian. He believed that God was Lord of all. He accepted the account in the first books of the Bible, the Pentateuch, that God had created the world and all living creatures. He believed that, either through natural laws or by miraculous intervention, God prevented the stars from falling in on one another. God also corrects the irregularities of the solar system caused by comets and the orbits of planets. The laws of nature, themselves Newton believed the creation of God, could be corrected and changed by the action of God. It was never Newton's intention to undermine belief in the Christian God. He was himself a keen theologian, albeit he was also interested in alchemy and ancient chronology. His followers have used his arguments as reason to believe in God's rational design of nature. From the above account it may seem as though Newton was a deist. Gay maintains that Newton could not have been a deist. He would not have kept his Cambridge Chair, nor had a subsequent successful government career, if he had not been theologically orthodox. Newton's scientific discoveries were never at the expense of his Christian faith.

There is no need to make too much of this. My intention is not to kidnap Newton for a Christian cause. But we can note that Newton exemplifies, and no more than this, the combination of a scientific mentality with an ongoing belief in God. Newton's theological studies do not hold a place in the discipline in any way comparable with his scientific work. In fact, the theology is neglected and obscure. But Newton is, despite the alchemy and pre-critical reading of the Pentateuch, a modern man. He could even be thought of as a modern Western secular man. That is, he was someone who was possessed of a scientific mind and a set of religious beliefs.

If Newton was the heroic genius of the Enlightenment, then its most significant project was the *Encyclopédie*. The work consisted of some 17 volumes of text and 11 of plates.[18] The majority of the volumes were published between 1750 and 1763. Its main architect was Diderot, although he was assisted initially by d'Alembert. Diderot devoted most of his life to this vast storehouse of knowledge. The *Encyclopédie* embodied the essence of the Enlightenment dream. It was the gathering together of as much technological knowledge as possible. A vast army of contributors wrote articles for its pages. Its criteria for inclusion, at least overtly, were whatever was scientific, by which was meant anything that was empirical. Its purpose was twofold. It was designed to combat traditional and outmoded belief and practice. And it was meant to disseminate new knowledge as far and wide as possible. This would enable ever newer discoveries, building on the exciting developments of enlightenment scientists. It was expensive, but even so the *Encyclopédie* sold 4,000 copies and was widely disseminated throughout France.

Despite the intention, the volumes of the *Encyclopédie* were not limited merely to an examination of scientific fact. Amongst its pages the spirit of the age was debated and discussed. So there were excursions into politics, religion and philosophy. The radical and controversial views expressed in these articles were necessarily buried to avoid the critical eyes of the government censors. The sheer number of contributors meant a certain amount of diversity of opinion. Much of the opinion was of high quality since amongst the contributors were not only Diderot and d'Alembert, but also, for example, Montesquieu, whose ideas in turn the *Encyclopédie* helped to publicize. The dominant ethos of enlightenment ensured an overriding consensus in the many articles. They reflected the spirit of the age. Gay believes that its range of material exploring arts and crafts, philosophy, politics, theology and language, to say nothing of the science, was evidence of the 'recovery of nerve, of the variety, wealth, and energy of eighteenth-century civilization'.[19] The purpose of the project, according to Diderot, was to change people's opinions and thereby to change their lives. For many, this is precisely what occurred. What they learnt, and what the conveyer belt of volumes represented, was the scientific mentality of the Enlightenment. It was to science and its practitioners, not the Church and its myths and superstitions, that they should now turn.

The scientific mentality emerged and triumphed at the Enlightenment. This is not to say that there were not signs and precursors in earlier ages. But after the Enlightenment, there was no turning back. The new science – that is, mathematics, empiricism, observation and experiment – had won the battle against deductive reasoning, superstition, myths and metaphysics. The latter would remain amongst the old-fashioned scientists, amongst some philosophers and widely amongst the population at large. But science would not return to those methods for its factual statements. Observation led to knowledge. Evidence, if it was to be accepted, was empirical. Any interpretation of empirical evidence was just that: interpretation. And interpretation could be challenged by the facts. Science was no longer theological and it was not philosophical in any sort of Cartesian sense. Science had grown up and abandoned its superstitions. Even the most speculative sciences, the science of modern cosmology or quantum physics, is to be validated by what can be known through observation and experiment. And this is beyond the experience of most people. For most people in the West, the scientific mentality dominates. Voltaire was right: we are all Newton's disciples.

The Anti-Christianity of the Enlightenment

Our previous discussion of Isaac Newton's Christian faith raises the more general question of the amount of anti-Christian feeling during the Enlightenment. To what extent was Newton the exception or the norm? Did the philosophes share his beliefs or, as is more widely supposed, was the Enlightenment a time when Christianity and the Church was widely and viciously attacked. What we shall see is that it is undoubtedly the case that important philosophes severely criticized the Church. They highlighted its absurdities and attacked its dogmatism, but they were not fundamentally opposed to the idea of religious belief. They sometimes saw a role for a type of civil religion, although this was in the context of a pluralist, free, cosmopolitan society.

The philosophes frequently condemned the Church. In France, Spain and Italy, this meant the Roman Catholic Church. In England, Holland, Germany and other Western European countries, it was more complex as a number of Protestant churches coexisted. However, as in England, there was sometimes a state Church to attack. The French were the most vitriolic.[20] In the words of Professor Roy Porter, they expended great energy 'habitually satirizing priests as perverts, friars as gluttons, monks and nuns as lechers, theologians as hair-splitters, inquisitors as sadistic torturers, and Popes as megalomaniacs'. The reason for the venom was that the Church was the enemy of enlightenment. The philosophes believed that the Church was deliberately engaged in the systematic suppression of ordinary people. People were kept ignorant and superstitious by a corrupt and hypocritical Church. It used its doctrines to reinforce its power. The Church taught unscientific nonsense about miracles, and threatened children and the gullible with the torments of hell and purgatory to bolster its political power. This it could do because it controlled so many schools. It deceived young men and women into monasteries and convents. It condemned as heretical and pagan all those who disagreed with its teaching. This had substantially restricted the development of scientific thought through the persecution of Galileo. This alone was sufficient a crime to ignite the ferocious anger of the philosophes. But, added to this, the Church wanted to restrict freedom of thought and expression. This was the cardinal sin in the eyes of the Enlightenment intellectuals. They could not countenance an organization that claimed it already had the truth.

So Montesquieu called the Pope a magician; Hume unpicked the traditional arguments in favour of the existence of God; Gibbon blamed Christians for the demise of the glorious Roman civilization. Of all those who attacked the Church, perhaps Voltaire is the most famous. He was ever armed with a cutting quip with which to harass the Church. He took up the notorious Calas case. The Calas family were Protestants. Their older son was found dead and it was rumoured that his father had killed him because he was about to convert to Roman Catholicism, the disgrace of the conversion being more than the family could bear. The father was tried and found guilty. Voltaire supposed him innocent, but either way what the case exposed was the insidious impact of Christian sectarianism. The religion of peace led to either a father killing his son or a man falsely executed. For Voltaire, it demonstrated the bigotry and violence of the Church.

Voltaire's masterpiece of anti-Church rhetoric was the fable *Candide*. It was an attack on the leading Christian philosopher/theologian Leibniz. Leibniz is caricatured in tale as the ridiculous figure of the tutor Dr Pangloss. As Candide travels and suffers one gross misfortune after another, he constantly returns to Pangloss' vacuous platitude that 'everything is for the best'. Gay describes *Candide* as a secular morality tale. The central character, the young man Candide, travels so swiftly from one cruelty to another that we are not tempted to believe the story was meant to be realistic; but neither is the world Candide encounters in any way enchanted. Life is portrayed as cruel and dangerous, people are full of greed, lust and trickery, and nature has a habit of inflicting great pain. Candide is a witness to the Lisbon earthquake, which had such an impact on eighteenth-century society, and he also witnesses the crude superstitions which follow the tragedy. In all of this realism there is no place for magic or mystery. It is a tale devoid of prayer and superstition. At the end of the tale, Candide accepts the limited nature of human experience. Gay offers a full interpretation of the final sentence in the novel, the concluding reflection on Candide's experience. In response to Pangloss' metaphysical speculation, Candide replies: 'That's well said, but we must cultivate our garden':

> Here, in the concluding sentence of the tale, Voltaire
> has fused the lessons of ancient philosophy into a

prescription: Men are thrown into the world to suffer and to dominate their suffering. Life is a shipwreck, but we must not forget to sing in the lifeboats; life is a desert, but we can transform our corner into a garden. Talk is entertaining, but it is useful only when it directs us to our duties and possibilities, since action is irresponsible without a clear conception of duty and unrealistic without a fair appreciation of our possibilities. It is the task of philosophy to discover, as the Stoics said long ago, what is within our power and what is beyond it. Candide is thus a morality tale in the most concrete sense possible: it teaches, by example, the supremacy of realistic moral thinking.[21]

By the final stages of his life, Voltaire was an atheist. The Lisbon earthquake of 1755 destroyed what notions he had of the benign God of creation. The death and suffering of that natural disaster made it hard for him to accept a benevolent Designer behind Nature. Others travelled a similar journey to atheism via deism. Like Voltaire, they were able to use classical philosophy as a tool with which to critique the Church and Christianity.

What is interesting is that despite the severity of the attacks on the Church, and despite individual examples of atheism, as a whole the philosophes did not advocate the end of all religion. It is possible to overstate the antipathy that was felt towards the notion of religious belief. This is not to say the Church was not subject to attack, of course it was. But many philosophes could discern a place in society for a form of civil religion. This was the viewpoint of Gibbon, who recognized its value in Roman times, and, for a while, Voltaire. Famously, Voltaire thought religion was good for the servants and one's wife in ensuring the maintenance of moral standards. This type of civil religion was not meant to be Christian. Others, like Rousseau and Priestly, seemed to have a more spiritual conception of religion. What this means is that, despite the famous instances of Voltaire's polemic or Hume's scepticism, it would be wrong to think of the Enlightenment as solely a time of atheism and irreligion. The picture was more complex, even as the new scientific mentality triumphed.

The Christian Identity of Liberal Ethics

So far we have argued that the major impact of the Enlightenment on contemporary thought was the emergence of a scientific mentality. This was at the expense of Christian doctrine. The scientific mentality surpassed Christianity as the functional technology of the modern period. Alongside this development, it was as a result of the Enlightenment that liberalism emerged as the ethical system which dominates contemporary Western society. There are questions which are asked of liberalism, such as those raised by post-modern scholars, which I shall examine in the final chapter. But my argument is that for most people liberalism remains the most important ethical ideology. In this section, I shall argue that liberalism has strong roots in Christian theology and these roots continue to shape its modern form. In particular, I shall argue first that individualism makes sense because of its Christian history. Then I shall look at key liberal ideas, such as the notions of progress, hope and humanism, and argue that these are expressions of Christianity. What this amounts to is the idea that liberalism is an expression of secular Christianity. The ethics which derive from liberalism are the form Christianity adopts in secular Western society.

The relationship between the moral identity of Western society and Christianity has been investigated by political theorists, in particular Professor Larry Siedentop and Professor John Gray.[22] Siedentop recognizes that the claim that Christianity shapes the ethics of modern Western society may seem an 'odd claim'. He recognizes, as we must, that great political philosophers such as Hobbes and Hume through to John Stuart Mill were anti-clerical and anti-religious. What is suggested here is no attempt to Christianize these writers. But it is an attempt to understand the philosophical and religious framework which allowed them to think as they did.

At the heart of Western culture is the notion of the individual. This idea stems from a belief that the individual human being is able to exercise his or her own moral will. The individual has a status which means they as individuals can make moral and ethical decisions. The existence of an individual moral will is the product of the amalgamation of Christianity with a Hellenistic concern with universals, and with the Jewish priority of conforming to God's will. Christianity introduced the notion that we are all radically equal. People are children of God. This was not the case in classical society. As a result of the integration of Judaism, Hellenism and Christianity, the relationship between humanity and the divine became personal rather than tribal. The Christian focus on the response of the individual to the divine will set up not only a new personal relationship with God, but eventually a new set of social relations. In Siedentop's words, 'the Christian conception of God provided the foundation for what became an unprecedented type of human society', by which he means democracy. This was a different type of democracy to the classical era because of the fundamental equality which underpinned its ideology.

Western individualism is at the very least 'residual Christianity'. It may be more than this because it may be reformed Christianity. The Christian God survives in the assumption that we can function as individuals. That is, we assume that humans have, as a right, the capacity to access the truth. We can understand and investigate the nature of reality as individuals, not as a tribe or society. Our conscience and our personal judgments have a status because of our individualism. We have equal liberty and equal rights because we have individual and universal moral status. These individual rights make it possible for society to function as a democracy. And in the West, the ethical status of democracy is unchallenged, whatever the failings and imperfections of its practice.

The question is then: how do we explain the anti-Church sentiment of secularism and also the pluralism of modern society? Siedentop argues that during the Middle Ages the Church had become accustomed to a powerful political position in society. As such, it lost its conviction in human equality. It therefore resisted the attempts of those in the eighteenth century to turn the notion of radical – what was called natural – equality back on the Church. As he says, the 'vision of equal liberty, which the Church had in fact nourished, was then turned against the Church itself'.[23] The Church was a bastion of the social elitism and conservative hierarchies which it had originally challenged in the name of equality. The fact that most people are no longer normally churchgoers, nor concerned with matters of Christian theology, should not obscure the fact that Western liberalism makes sense because of its Christian roots. Where the Church suffers from aggressive liberal attack, it is in the name of a Christian theology it has forgotten. Such attacks urge a return to the basic Christian conviction that humans are moral individuals capable of exercising choice.

In his discussion of pluralism, Siedentop draws a distinction between individual pluralism and group pluralism. The latter, when it results in the restriction of individual liberty, is ethically rejected by Western society. A group which argued that all its left-handed members should be denied an education would be subject to moral condemnation in the West. Such a group has denied the individual a fundamental right. In individual pluralism, the individual is given ethical status through the right to exercise choice. So if an individual chose to deny themselves a post-compulsory education because they were left-handed, then this might be criticized as abnormal and ill-judged; but its moral status would stand. The aim would be to change the individual's judgment rather than deny the right of the individual to exercise the choice.

What this means is that Western notions of (individual) pluralism, of tolerance, and even of scepticism, are not negative beliefs but the product of a Christian culture. To argue that they are negative beliefs is to miss a crucial part of Western history:

It misses the fact that Western distinctions between the
state and civil society, public and private spheres, mere
conformity and moral conduct are themselves derived
from Christian assumptions. That is, they rest on a
framework of assumptions and valuations which can be
described broadly as individualist and which correspond
in crucial respects to the framework of Christian
theology. The assumption that society consists of
individuals, each with an ontological ground of his or
her own, is a translation of the Christian premise of
equality of souls in the eyes of God. That fundamental
equality of status which Christianity postulates
became, especially through the Natural Law tradition,
the means by which Western thinkers from the Middle
Ages into the modern period drew an increasingly
systematic distinction between the person as moral
agent and the social roles which such persons happened
to occupy.[24]

This means that 'Christian ontology provided the founda-
tion for what are usually described as liberal values in the
West'. In one sense, what is argued here should be no surprise.
A society which emerges out of a Christian past should be
expected to display signs of that past in its ongoing life.
However, the surprise is that Western society has frequently
believed that it rejected its Christian past. The advent of
secularism, especially in its liberal form, was the removal of
Christianity. The argument here is that Christianity persists.
It persists in the ideology which was supposed to have
replaced it. Furthermore, because of the radical equality in
Christianity, expressed in the universal notion that all people
are moral agents (i.e. all people are individuals), then liberalism is but a different form of Christianity. The ethical identity
of Western society will remain discernibly Christian for as
long as the individual has higher moral status than the group.
   The same point about the Christian identity of Western
liberalism can be made in a different way. What we have

examined so far concentrated on the underlying structure of Western liberalism and its Christian identity. Another approach would be to take features of liberalism and relate them to elements of Christian theology. This is John Gray's approach.[25] He does it by arguing for a nihilist understanding of humanity. This brings to the fore the Christian presuppositions of many commonly held Western views. For example, the humanist belief in progress, the notion that humanity can grow in scientific knowledge and thereby increase its power over nature, is but a secular version of the Christian idea that salvation is open to everyone. It depends on the equally Christian notion that human beings are different from other animals. They have a special status. But since Darwin, we know this is not the case. And in a post-Darwinian world the notion of progress is an illusion.[26] This is because it only makes sense to speak of humans surviving through evolution. This is not progress, it is survival or evolution.

Likewise, the notion that knowledge of the truth will set humanity free is a myth. Modern faith in truth, not least scientific truth, is an ancient creed originating in Socrates. This faith was passed on to Plato, via Plato to Christianity, and then on to humanist and scientific thought. Modern humanism is the belief that through science humanity can know the truth. But, as Gray states, 'if Darwin's theory of natural selection is true this is impossible. The human mind serves evolutionary success, not truth'. Humans are built to pass on genes, not investigate the truth of anything. In fact, evolution prospers better when engaged in self-deception. The self-deception that believes 'I will love this person for ever' can be used to make convincing promises which help attract a mate. All of this adds to Gray's conclusion that humanism is a 'secular religion thrown together from decaying scraps of Christian myth'.[27]

The essence of humanism's mistake is that it believes humans are different from other animals. In this it follows Christianity. Christians believe they are special because they are uniquely created and saved by God, and can exercise free will. Humanists believe they are special because they are self-determining. But this presupposes an individual will and this, Gray argues, is an illusion. Individuality is an illusion. The notion of a conscious identity is but the product of conflicts amongst our impulses. Gray argues that the notion of coherent identity is a construct, whereby a central controlling 'person' is posited to give order to what are fragmentary and competing behaviours. What is important here is that to get away from humanism and thereby to escape Christianity, the very concept of the individual has to be abandoned.

Gray's book is an exposition of a Darwinian worldview for animals, including human beings. As such, it will be no surprise that he believes that 'moral philosophy is very largely a branch of fiction'.[28] The notion that morality is superior as a way of life to immorality or cooking comes from the classical world and from Christianity. It has an unquestioned status as the most desirable way to live. It is better to be moral than evil. But in the animal kingdom the good life can often be something Western Christians and humanists call immoral. In fact, human beings are killers. They are not the worst in the animal kingdom, nor are they entirely unrestrained, but they are killers. The idea that morality rules the world and that in history, even if individual sacrifice is required, still the good will win out is a Christian myth.

The purpose of these examples is not to make a case for Gray's version of nihilism. It is rather to illustrate the pervasive presence of Christian liberal ethics in Western society. Much of what Gray argues has effect because it is shocking. But that in itself illustrates our argument that Christian theology in the form of ethics is fully immersed in and adopted by Western society. The effort of liberalism to resist Christianity has failed. Gray's efforts are more successful. But then we are forced to describe his ideas as 'nihilist', as though the absence of Christian liberal ethics is actually the absence of ethics in its entirety. This is possible only because it is so difficult to imagine an alternative to identifiably Christian ethics. For most people such an effort is not required or expected. They live within the bounds of Christian ethics.

In this chapter, we have argued that liberal ethics has a Christian identity because of its fundamental individualism. We have further seen the pervasive presence of Christian ethics in Western society through an exploration of a nihilist alternative. What this means is that when the secular West seeks to be ethical it still draws on Christian ideas and sources. Christianity has an ongoing presence within Western secular society. This Christian ethics coexists with a scientific mentality. This arose during the Enlightenment period, largely as a result of the remarkable innovations of Isaac Newton. His views were popularized by Voltaire and adopted by social scientists, philosophers, medics and natural scientists. The Enlightenment was often anti-clerical and anti-Church but, as we have seen, Christian ideas survived the shift to humanism. So as we approach the contemporary period, we have a notion of modern people with the capacity to hold together two sets of beliefs. In their technology they were scientific and in their ethics they were Christian. The question is: why is Western society thought of as secular when it is made up of scientific Christians? To answer this, we must investigate the Victorian period.

Chapter Eight

The Last Puritan Age

In his important study of religious life in Britain during the last 200 years, Callum Brown describes the Victorian era as the 'nation's last puritan age'.[1] During the nineteenth century Britain was a 'deeply Christian country', with remarkably high levels of churchgoing and a culture which promoted exceptional standards of individual moral conduct. In this chapter, I shall explore the evidence for this claim. The contemporary story of Church decline stems from comparing twentieth-century churchgoing with that of the Victorian period. This is a comparison between a relatively normal period of Church allegiance, our own time, with one that stands out for its high levels. As such, the story of decline is unavoidable and, if it is assumed the Church's demise will surely follow, unfair.

I shall also examine two further points that inform our understanding of Christian life today and are related to the Victorian period. The first is the failure of atheism. This is demonstrated by the chequered history of secular societies. Secularism as an organized force developed during the nineteenth century. It has not, however, been able to make a major impact on British cultural life. The second is ongoing belief in God. The oft-quoted statistical evidence shows how persistent belief in God is. What is important about this for my study is twofold. First, we need to be aware that a number of important nineteenth-century thinkers sought to challenge belief in God. Second, there is a close connection between ethics and belief in God. Friedrich Nietzsche, one of the prophets of God's death, argues this point. He suggests that the death of God has led to the collapse of ethical values. In the West, the opposite has happened. Western society combines an ongoing belief in the existence of God with a commitment to thinking and talking in public about ethics. This will lead to the proposition that Christianity in the West is of central importance because we live in what can be called the ethics society. The proposition will then be explored in the final chapter.

Christianity in the Victorian Era

The starting point for my investigation into Christian belief and practice during the Victorian period is the statistical data. I have already mentioned Horace Mann's 1851 Census of Religious Worship, but it bears reiterating. Around about 60 per cent of the population of England, Scotland and Wales were recorded as being in church on census Sunday. To find the absolute number of people in the population who attended church, the figure has to be lowered. This takes account of a large number who went to church twice. Even so, the most conservative estimates suggest at least a third of the popula- tion was in church.[2] More generous estimates calculate the figure at between 40 and 50 per cent. This is an exceptionally high figure. It could be even higher if we add to the number those regular attendees who will have missed the census Sunday because of illness or unavoidable commitments.

The majority of those who attended church were women.[3] This had an impact on churchgoing patterns. If the household were wealthy enough to have servants, then the women attended in the morning. Domestics servants and those too poor to have hired help attended in the evening. This was because Sunday lunch was so important. If women had to cook the meal themselves, then they were unable to attend the mid-morning services. Instead, they went in the evening along with the servants who had been preparing the meal. Brown also argues, against scholars such as Professor Hugh McLeod, that working class attendance was higher than previously thought. The exception to this was the unskilled working classes, although this may have been because they went to unrecorded services such as mid-week worship or irregular religious gatherings.

The question these figures raise is: why were so many people in church? To answer this, we need to take a step back and look at how the evidence of religious practice has been gathered. We shall see that the statistical data provides a very limited picture of religious belief and practice. When we have a fuller picture of what was going on, then we shall see the major effort that was made to attract people to church. But first, we need to start with the question of how religious behaviour is monitored and assessed.

Callum Brown has argued that there is a problem with the way in which Christian belief and practice is measured.[4] The overriding emphasis has been on counting the number of people in church at services. This has the effect of superficially dividing people into one of two polar opposites. People are either churchgoers or they are not. They are either believers or they are not. Such results, and the categories they generate, lack any nuance given the wide variety of people's religious commitments. It is also a highly institutional approach to religion. Attending church becomes the only mode by which people can express their Christian faith. This might be what the Church itself advocates. It may also suit those wishing to study Christian behaviour, since it is a simple means of accumulating hard evidence. But religious life is not so easily reduced to such empirical measures. What figures for church-going tell us is roughly how many people are likely to be in church – week by week or month by month. This is not the same as telling us how much allegiance people feel towards the Church or what importance Christian beliefs have in their lives. Even if we add figures for baptisms, weddings and funerals or attendance at Sunday school, we still do not get a full picture of belief and practice. For this, a much more subtle approach is required.

Added to this problem is a second dilemma. We need to be suspicious about the people who wanted to measure church-going. Gathering the statistics was not a disinterested science. The Victorians who commissioned the studies and gathered the evidence had an agenda which motivated their work. What they sought to do was illustrate a Church in decline. Horace Mann, when presenting his report on church attendance to Parliament, did not celebrate the remarkably high figures.[5] Instead, he spoke of 'the alarming numbers of non-attendants' at church. In particular, he pointed out the absence of working class-people in congregations. He argued that the working classes were as unaware of religious teaching as people in 'heathen countries'. In this, Mann agreed with Thomas Chalmers, who, in 1815, had moved from a rural parish to minister in Glasgow. Chalmers worked vigorously to collect information on churchgoing patterns. From this, he constructed a picture of the godless city. It was an image of the city as a great mass of pagan and heathen humanity. The population, especially the poor, were unchurched and, more worryingly for the dominant social class, dangerously immoral. Chalmers achieved national fame through his study of the religious state of the city. He was mobbed on a visit to London in 1817. His work was almost universally referred to in discussions of churchgoing census material. The heathen city was the dominant myth of the nineteenth century. The studies of churchgoing, not least of which was Horace Mann's, added to this picture.

But why would people want to create alarm about the Christian state of the population? To answer this, we need to look at who was complaining about the low figures. The first and main group were the clergy of the established Church. They felt threatened. They were in danger of losing the power that came with their status. In particular, they feared the rise of nonconformity. Nonconformist churches were growing and, as the century progressed, their members were being granted full political rights. Church of England clergy saw the rise of nonconformity as a threat to the parish church system. People had the option of leaving the established Church, of going to do their own thing. For parish clergy this was unacceptable. They often equated nonconformity with godlessness. They wanted to draw people back into their congregations and stoking up fears about godlessness would help this aim.

Of lesser concern, but nevertheless prevalent, was the fear that atheism and religious apathy were rising. The number of atheists and secularists never reached the levels or influence of the nonconformists, but they were part of a picture in which clergy could see their standing diminished and their power decline. They needed to start warning people about the perilous state of churchgoing before the situation got any worse.

The second influential group who felt threatened by changing patterns of religious behaviour were local landowners. The Church of the eighteenth century had been closely allied with the land. Clergy gentlemen, not unknown to the novels of Jane Austin, shared the civilized preoccupations and manners of the local gentry. They were often in their employ and frequently taken from their families. The shift of large numbers of people to the cities with the rise of industrialization, combined with the growth of Methodism and other nonconformist churches, alarmed those used to traditional ways. It broke the link between landowner, church and local community. The social hierarchy, physically represented by who sits where in the church, was under threat. The local gentry were not happy with the breakdown of the rituals and rites of the local community, of which church attendance was an important example, if it undermined the deference and obedience they might expect throughout the working week. They themselves would complain about the decline in Christian belief and they would encourage their clergy to do the same.

What was in the interests of both these groups were a set of results which inspired and motivated good Christian people to redouble their efforts to bring the local heathen back into church. The statistical data provided these results. The numbers counted not only provided a partial assessment of Christian belief and practice, but also set out to confirm a pre-existing picture. This is not to say that results were deliberately falsified, which is most unlikely. But it is to say that when seeking to examine Victorian Christianity, those who were leading the research desired and expected a picture that was pessimistic. A comprehensive account of Christianity was not the factor which motivated the research. It was not the intention to demonstrate the variety of ways in which people lived out their Christian faith. The aim of the research was to show the reduction in importance of the parish church. However, the fears expressed by the clergy and social elite about the Christian life of the urban population were unfounded. There is plenty of evidence of a remarkable amount of Christian belief and practice. In fact, the widespread concern about churchgoing was itself a sign that Christianity had an important role in society. When actual secularization occurred, then it would only be the minority left in church who would care. They, because of their diminished status, would find it hard to draw anyone else in to share their worries.

In response to this problem of measuring belief and practice, Callum Brown employs an alternative to what he describes as the reductionist social science methodology which has dominated debates about secularization. He looks for a wider range of sources which reveal people's religious sensibility. For example, he is interested in what popular literature, novels, magazines and religious tracts tell us about personal beliefs. The testimonies of people in diaries, autobiographies, obituaries and interviews give us a sense of the religious climate of the time. In these testimonies, people report the informal aspects of their religious practices. That is the saying of grace before meals, forms of Sabbath observance and the singing of hymns on a Sunday evening. Alongside this, the publications and utterances of the institutional Church have a place. They will reflect back to the population, and thereby the researcher, the concerns clerics have about the religious life of the time. The picture generated from such wide-ranging and diffuse evidence will not be as precise as a figure produced by a statistical survey. In some instances, complex or contradictory patterns will emerge. But then our expectation is that people's religious allegiances and beliefs are generally messy. What is being investigated is the multifarious personal, religious and social identity of human beings.[6]

All of which takes me back to the question of why so many people were going to church during the Victorian period. One value of the methodology proposed by Brown is that it accounts for the high levels of churchgoing. What it shows is the importance of a strong religious culture. In a free society people cannot be forced into church. There is a tendency to suppose that people go to church solely because of their private beliefs. That is, someone who believes in God will attend church because it is a logical consequence of their belief. If they do not go to church then their profession is suspect. But this is a simplistic picture of how and why church attendance occurs. A major influence on people will be the social and cultural environment in which they live. This might consist of overt social pressure or it might be the result of an intense religious culture which people find hard to ignore or resist. What we shall see is that the Christian culture of the Victorian period was widespread and enormously influential. It was this diffuse and pervasive culture which shepherded large sections of the population into church. It combined with an enormous evangelizing effort to produce the high levels of churchgoing which was characteristic of the times.

The Godly Life

During the Victorian period, remarkable efforts were made to convert the people of Britain to Christ. The nineteenth century was a time of intense, organized and strategic evangelization. Brown summarizes the situation well:

From 1796 to 1914, Britain was immersed in the greatest exercise in Christian proselytism this country has ever seen. It focused the individual on personal salvation and ideals of moral behaviour and manifestations of outward piety. It reconstructed the local church in its modern form – not a parish state of regulatory courts, church discipline and landowner power, but the congregation as a private club and a parliament of believers. And it spawned the 'associational ideal' by which true believers could express their conversion in the assurance shown through commitment to evangelizing work in voluntary organizations.[7]

There are two points to be noted here. First is Brown's argument that at the beginning of the nineteenth century evangelicalism took the notion of the individual and turned it into the focus for salvation. What this means is that evangelicals prompted the individual to make a personal decision about their faith. This was necessary to be saved. It was not enough to belong to the parish. This choice of salvation was then made manifest in the individual's behaviour. Whether Brown is correct about the timing here is controversial. However, it is not significant for our argument. What is significant is the next point. From the Victorian age onwards, underpinned by the culture of individual salvation, an organized, vigorous effort was made to bring people to church. Alongside this was a concurrent campaign to ensure people were sober, clean, hard-working, faithful in marriage and abstemious out of it. In other words, the reason so many people went to church during the Victorian era was that they were subject to an intense campaign of Christian propaganda. People were urged to live godly lives. The culture in which they lived bombarded them with the message that they must be godly, and to be godly they must be clean, sober and churchgoing.

There were three main tools used to create the culture of godly living. These were the Sunday school, tract distribution and local visiting. Each of these grew during the Victorian period. They were supported by the committed congregation who would provide the funds and personnel to ensure their successful operation. The congregation was more like a voluntary club eager to attract new members and promote its life. Sunday schools were the first of these three developments in church life. They emerged during the late eighteenth century. The resilience of the schools was remarkable. As late as the mid-twentieth century a majority of children attended schools, and the memories of recent generations' Sundays is one of afternoons in class.

More interesting for our purposes are home visiting and tract distribution. Home visiting developed during the first half of the nineteenth century. Its scope and efforts are stunningly impressive. A number of agencies were employed to do the work. The London City Mission is an example of one major agency:

> In 1863, the London City Mission was reported as having 380 paid agents who closed 203 shops on Sundays. They made 2,012,169 home visits during the year at which the Scriptures were read 579,391 times. They distributed 9,771 copies of the Bible and 2,970,527 tracts, and held 46,126 indoor meetings. They 'induced' 1,483 persons to become communicants of Christian churches, 619 families to begin family worship, and 360 cohabiting couples to marry; and 'saved from ruin' some 619 'fallen ones', presumably women.[8]

This is but one example. The whole operation was enormous. It was also very well planned. The agents would target individuals by age or gender or occupation. They would visit places of 'sin', such as public houses, betting premises and shops open on a Sunday. This required a certain degree of courage or faithfulness. Homes were visited in a systematic manner. Visitors would be assigned streets and houses and were asked to record what they found. This could range from the clean, friendly and pious to the dirty, drunkard and immoral. The latter can hardly have been pleased to receive the visit. When the visit was successful, then services would be held in the front room, tracts and Bibles distributed, and families encouraged to visit the local church.

The main consequence of this vast visiting programme was to promote Christianity in a way never attempted before or since. Church congregations grew as a result of the efforts of the faithful. Alongside this primary impact, it is worth noting an important side-effect. In a remarkable way the working classes and the poor opened up their homes to the evangelists. This is surprising to contemporary eyes. What it meant was an interaction between different elements of society. Sometimes this was between the pious and the 'fallen'. Sometimes the middle classes or prosperous working classes would be exposed to the lives of the poorest and most destitute. This cannot but have had an impact on the more sensitive of them.

One element of home visiting was the distribution of religious tracts. During the nineteenth century, tract publication and distribution became a vast undertaking. As an illustration, the Drummond Tract Enterprise in Scotland was established in 1848.[9] Within ten years the company had printed more than 200 publications and sold eight million copies. By the start of the First World War there were more than 300 different tracts, as well as novels, short stories, religious poems and children's books.

Tracts were distributed freely to aid conversion. There was a belief that tracts could reach parts of the nation from which even the most committed visitor was debarred. Miss V.M. Skinner distributed texts of scripture to public houses. Tracts were short, usually one piece of paper folded to produce either one, two or four pages. Those who distributed the tracts needed funds to purchase them from publishers. Typically, tracts included a short sermon, an attack on some social or personal evil and an exhortation to improve one's life. Sunday trading, gambling, drinking and 'living immorally' were unsurprising targets for criticism. Also, subjects for condemnation

were dance halls, theatres and ballrooms. These, whilst perhaps not as bad as public houses, were not places of serious
moral improvement.

There was advice on how to deliver a tract. It was not
appropriate to rush up and thrust a tract at someone before
leaving quickly. It was far better to make a casual approach,
read the tract oneself and then offer it to the person with a
warm recommendation. This could be along the lines of saying
that one has read the tract a number of times and believe the
stranger may profit from a similar reading. If this was too
time-consuming then a bright smile and a warm word, however brief, were the order of the day.

In addition to the short tract, there developed a healthy
market for magazines. Novels were normally serialized in
magazines. As the century progressed stories became more
popular, although they had had a place from the start. Tales
were told of those who succumbed to bad ends as a result of
immoral lives. Charles Cook visited prisons and used the stories he heard there as a basis for his tales of unfortunate people
suffering for their crimes. Equally, the rags-to-riches story,
based on hard work and resisting temptation, could teach a
valuable moral lesson. Efforts were made to integrate tales of
romance and religious improvement or adventure and morality.

What this combination of religious education, improving
literature and home visiting achieved was the Christianization
of a nation. This was not a matter of getting people to attend
church. Even by more generous estimates, one-half of the
population was not counted in church on census Sunday. It
was instead the creation of a Christian culture. Evangelical
Christianity dominated the discussion of what was good and
holy behaviour. The social and cultural expectations of what
constituted the moral and responsible person were defined by
Christianity and in particular evangelical Christianity. This
was as true for the Victorian political scene as it was in the
local community or the home. This does not mean everyone
agreed with the evangelicals. It does not mean everyone went
to church or lived a good life. But everyone shared the same

notion of what made up the moral life. If someone did not go to church or observe the Sabbath or drank excessively, then they knew, as did everyone else, that they were sinning in the sight of God and their fellow citizens.

One fascinating product of evangelical Christian culture, and one sign of its social strength, was the development of the idea of the good Christian woman. A good woman was a pillar of moral rectitude. She would be pious, devoted to churchgoing, prayer and the study of scripture. She would be domestic, keeping a well-ordered and clean house. She would be thrifty and hard working, loving towards her children and caring towards her husband. There would never be any questions asked about the propriety of her behaviour with the opposite sex. The moral woman could be assured of the respect of her peers and the rewards in the next life for her piety.

But the moral woman was also constantly under threat. The threat came from the bad man. This might be the drunkard, gambling husband or the wayward son. Poverty and destitution could be caused by the excesses of betting or drinking. A young woman, prior to marriage, might find herself deceived by the immoral suitor. It was the role and duty of the good woman to battle on in the face of the adversity caused by the bad man. It was also her duty to try and save him and bring him to holiness and right living. If all went well, then the man might be reformed and brought around to a life of piety, thrift, hard work and churchgoing.

These images of the good woman confronted by a man in need of redemption were extremely powerful. They pervaded culture and, according to Brown, were a controlling force in women's lives until the 1960s. How was it that they could be so dominant? Brown attributes the force to the extent to which such images were propagated in magazines and tracts. The stories told of heroic women were those of moral rectitude and courage. Obituaries celebrated the lives of women by recounting their deathbed praises of God. Evangelicalism developed a narrative structure, a formula, which controlled how good women were described. The way in which life itself was discussed was infiltrated by the morality that evangelical Christianity advocated. What is so impressive is the extent to which, in all areas of Victorian society and culture, this notion of morality was normal.

It was in this climate that exceptionally high numbers of people went to church. In light of the pressure this is hardly surprising. In fact, it is more surprising that so many were able to resist the social and cultural pressure. It was a unique operation that defined the times as one of Christian faith and churchgoing.

The Secular Society

It is interesting to note that a further consequence of this intense campaign of Christianization was the emergence of organized secularism. The contemporary usage of the term 'secular' dates from the mid-nineteenth century. In Britain, the Secular Society was founded in 1866 by Charles Bradlaugh.[10] He published a programme for a secular society, as well as conditions for membership, in the 9 September issue of the 'National Reformer'. Two weeks later the society was formed, with Bradlaugh as its President. However, this was not the first use of the term, nor was Bradlaugh the only architect of the movement.

Edward Royle, in his detailed study of British secularism, argues that the important architect of the movement was George Jacob Holyoake.[11] Bradlaugh is the more famous of the Victorian secularists because he was the first President of the national society and because of his well publicized failed attempts to enter Parliament. In 1880, Bradlaugh was elected Member of Parliament for Northampton, but he refused to take the religious Oath of Allegiance which was necessary if he was to take his seat. His constituency was therefore declared vacant and a by-election set up. Bradlaugh won the re-election contest on four occasions. It was only two years after he had entered Parliament in 1886, having taken the Oath, that the law was changed.

George Jacob Holyoake had done much to establish the society which Bradlaugh was to take over. In many ways, Holyoake was Bradlaugh's intellectual and political inferior. But Holyoake had developed the network of regional groups that made up mid-century secularism. These groups had emerged from the failures of the Owenite and Chartist movements. They were politically radical, and early secularism shared the socialist outlook. The disagreement between Bradlaugh and Holyoake was over the question of relations with Christian groups. Holyoake was more willing to work in cooperation with organizations such as the Christian Socialists. Bradlaugh was the more militant atheist. The two men finally split in 1862. Bradlaugh was the stronger and more organized leader who was to command greater support. Some regional groups did remain loyal to Holyoake.

The secularists were never able to grow into a mass movement attracting widespread support. This is not to deny that there were times of popularity at various points during the nineteenth century. Lectures and public meetings by well-known and engaging public speakers could attract large crowds. There was a market for the variety of publications that emerged from the leading members of the group. One of Holyoake's talents was in writing and editorship. But any hope of secularism developing into a mass working-class movement never materialized. Royle estimates that in the very widest sense there might have been about 100,000 sympathizers. Many of these, however, would have been Chartists who were not interested in secularism. The number of those concerned with secularism per se might have been as few as 20,000, and in the difficult years only half this number. The actual number of committed hardcore secularists who usually belonged and engaged with the movement was probably only about 3,000. At its peak in 1880, the National Secular Society had a membership of 6,000.[12] The contemporary position of secularism remains the same. The National Secular Society is a minority organization unable to attract much public attention or a significant number of members.

Royle concludes that secularism has a paradoxical legacy.[13] It never developed into a mass movement. In fact, it could barely be called a movement at all. Its early close links with Chartism probably account for the large numbers attending some of its meetings. Because those actually committed to the cause of secularism never amounted to more than a few thousand, it should be thought of as a small sect rather than a movement. The Secular Society never began to challenge the Church in terms of membership or power. It could never equal its evangelization efforts in money or personnel.

However, the picture is not entirely one of failure. Whilst the organization is small, nevertheless the subject of secularism and the concerns of secularists have often been at the forefront of public attention. Its issues continue to provoke discussion and debate throughout society. This has been the case with the question of blasphemy laws. Schools are another oft revisited area of dispute. It is also apparent that discussions are widespread if the core topic of whether there is a God or not is considered. Royle concludes that, whilst secularists have not been able to organize into an effective movement, nevertheless their desire to promote secularism as a topic for debate in the public square has been a success.

It is beyond the remit of this study to examine why such a paradox exists. It is only necessary to state that consistently a vast majority of people have affirmed their belief in God. Whilst this is the case and the secular organization is atheist, then we should not expect the movement to grow. It could be argued that this is a very simple explanation. The reasons are likely to be more complex than this. It may be that, as some argue, secularism is too dry and intellectual for most people. It lacks a ritual and emotional appeal that will draw people in and hold them. But even if something like this is the case, or another explanation is advanced, nevertheless secularism as a militant organization has not succeeded. This is one good reason to reassess why people continue to call Western society secular. What the failure of the secular movement demonstrates is that the designation 'secular' when applied to

Western society is not meant to describe people's atheist commitments. In fact, what the history of organized secularism reveals, and it is a point confirmed by contemporary secular groups, is that a meaningful description of secularism, if it is meant to apply to Western society, must entail a new definition of the term.

The Death of God

At a popular level, Victorian society was inundated with propaganda about the moral and pious life. The combined effect of home visits and tract distribution achieved their goal of getting large numbers of people to church. At an intellectual level, however, Christianity faced a number of serious challenges. What is interesting is that these developed at a period when Church allegiance was so high. We shall briefly examine some of these challenges before concentrating on the particular issue of the death of God, as proclaimed by Friedrich Nietzsche. Nietzsche's work concerns us because of the link he makes between belief in God and ethics.

What is interesting about the intellectual challenges to Christianity which emerged from the nineteenth century is the extent to which the Church has accepted and adopted many of the arguments made. On many occasions, what should have been atheism's killer blow has merely resulted in renewed and reformed Christianity. This shows that Christians take these challenges seriously. But it also shows the resilience of the process of ongoing inculturation described by Wessels.

I shall look at the ideas of Karl Marx and Charles Darwin below. The most dangerous threat to the Church came not from these thinkers, but from the unlikely source of biblical studies. In particular, the work of German scholars, of which the Tübingen School is the most important. Biblical scholars forced the Church to look again at its foundational texts. Scholars found these texts were not to be treated as though they were accurate historical records of the events described. What scholarship revealed was that when Christians read the Bible they should not regard it as the literal truth. For example, Moses' authorship of the first books of the Old Testament was called into question by the analysis of diverse genres of writing. These came from separate historical periods and cultural and religious backgrounds. The differences in the accounts of the Gospels came to be attributed to the varying motivations and contexts of the writer and his community. Questions were asked about the historical veracity of the miracle stories. All of which was a serious threat to the Church. If the Bible was not an accurate history, then could it be considered true? And if it was not true, then was not Christianity called in to doubt. What is remarkable is that many Christians were happy to accept the work of historical criticism and adapt their interpretation of the meaning of the Bible accordingly. Much of the mainstream Church, particularly liberal Christianity, was prepared to adopt these academic insights and transform its appreciation of Scripture. Of course, some Christians are determined to insist that the Bible should be treated as literal truth. In these cases, inculturation between historical criticism and Christianity has not occurred. But this does not mean a different inculturation is not at work. The point here is that Christianity had the capacity to respond to a major threat to its faith through a historical dissection of its foundation documents and it has survived. In some instances Christians thrived on the challenge. This is a challenge which is ongoing, as more analysis of biblical history and texts occurs.

The Victorian period is also well known for the conflict between science and religion. I have discussed this in relation to Freud in Chapter Two and have already described how Christians, like others in Western society, have adopted a scientific mentality. However, the point also needs to be made in relation to evolution, which, because of the US debate, is a special case. Charles Darwin's theory of evolution called into question the Christian account of creation as recorded in the book of Genesis. In the nineteenth century, Darwin was much ridiculed and attacked. There was also an intellectual response from the Church. Bishop Wilberforce famously challenged the theory at the 1860 debate at the meeting of the British Association for the Advancement of Science. Thomas Huxley made the case for evolution.

The debate about evolution has also taken a contemporary form. Richard Dawkins has utilized genetic science as the basis for his attacks on Christian belief. But we can easily agree with Steve Bruce that for most people the details of the theory, in either Darwin's original masterpiece or Dawkins' updating, have not been examined. Most Christians readily accept the theory of evolution as part of the scientific package whose advantages are technological.

The exception to this are those evangelical groups who argue that the theory of evolution has no more scientific grounding than the Genesis accounts of creation. These groups are mainly in the USA and their impact is insignificant in Western Europe. They advocate the teaching of creationism in schools either alongside evolution or instead of it. It could be argued that these groups reveal that Christians do take the detail of the theory of evolution seriously. This is true for a small number. However, even for the majority who support creationism, this comes as part of a socially conservative and anti-liberal package whose importance is not the detail of the debate, but the symbolic value of the stand. For those who want to promote a conservative agenda in the face of what they see as ever-increasing liberal dominance in the USA, then creationism is one belief amongst others such as anti-abortion legislation and same-sex marriage rights that demonstrates their position. In other words, the details of evolution gets caught up in a political campaign. This is not to denigrate the importance of the beliefs. Rather, it is to show that creationism does not mean these groups of evangelical Christians have resisted a scientific mentality.

The relationship between Marxism and Christianity is a second illustration of how the Church can adopt and transform political ideologies. Marxism is an atheist political ideology. Karl Marx's atheism was heavily influenced by Ludwig Feuerbach. Feuerbach understood belief in God to be a human construction. It was a projection of a human ideal onto a notion of the Divine. Feuerbach wanted to switch this process so that the study of theology became a study of humanity. Marx valued Feuerbach's desire to transform religion into an analysis of the human condition. Marx was critical of religious belief; however, he did not underestimate its social power. He argued that it was the way in which humanity expressed and coped with its state of alienation. The idea of human alienation was central to Marx's critique of capitalism and fundamental to his political philosophy. Alienation was the condition that resulted from people's exploitation under capitalism. For humanity to be able to achieve genuine fulfilment and happiness, they needed to abandon those beliefs and systems which created illusionary contentment. They were also to abandon capitalism, which was at the cause of the alienation.

What is important about Marx's ideas is not whether he is right about either religion or capitalism. What is remarkable is that some Christians could take a system which was fundamentally atheist and adopt it for their own purposes. More than this, a number of Christians have argued that Marxist analysis of the oppressive impact of capitalist society is a lesson the Church needs to learn. The Church has been culpable in colluding with capitalism through its support of conservative social orders. They would suggest the Church needs to repent of this past sin. The examples of Marxist theology include the rise of political theology in Germany in the 1960s and the advent of theologies of liberation in the 1970s. Theologies of liberation have been influential in the formation of a number of Christian movements such as Black Theology, Feminist Theology and Gay, Lesbian and Transgendered Theology. Of course, not all Christians have been happy about these developments nor agreed with their main points. Nor have Christians become atheists. But they have adopted the social, economic and political critique within Marxism and adapted their beliefs in light of its analysis. In this they illustrate an age-old process of inculturation which began with the Early Church and the shift from a Jewish context to the Hellenistic world. Christianity's capacity for self-reformation in light of new ideas and cultures is exceptional.

There seem to be almost no boundaries to this process of inculturation. It should be that by all normal definitions, Christians would be required to reject certain philosophies if they prove entirely incompatible with its beliefs. The philosophy of Friedrich Nietzsche might be expected to fall into this category. Nietzsche proclaimed the 'death of God'. Christianity is a theist faith which has a notion of a transcendent personal God at its heart. However, even the idea of the death of God was adopted and utilized by some theologians during the 1960s. This was not a precise adoption of Nietzsche; in particular, his ideas on Christian ethics were not employed, nor was the movement long lasting. There are only a few theologians who continue in this vein today, but the inculturation did occur. That it was not an especially influential or substantial movement is testament to the resilience of belief in God amongst a majority of people. The death-of-God theologies were attractive to intellectuals and some who were disillusioned with the Church in its traditional form.

This, however, is not the only reason Nietzsche is important for us. He also illustrates the connection between belief in God and ethics. In the next chapter we shall see how this connection is an ongoing feature of Western society. Nietzsche argued that the death of God entailed the destruction of social values and ethics. He did so through his famous and important parable of the madman. Despite its length, this parable is worth recalling. The parable appeared in *Gay Science*, published in 1882:

> *The Madman.* Have you not heard of that madman who lit a lantern in the bright morning hours, ran to the market place, and cried incessantly, 'I seek God! I seek God!' As many of those who did not believe in God were standing around just then, he provoked much laughter. Has he got lost? asked one. Did he lose his way

like a child? asked another. Or is he hiding? Is he afraid
of us? Has he gone on a voyage? or emigrated? This they
yelled and laughed.

The madman jumped in their midst and pierced them
with his eyes. 'Whither is God?' he cried. 'I shall tell
you. We *have killed him* – you and I. All of us are murder-
ers? But how did we do this? How could we drink up the
sea? Who gave us the sponge to wipe away the entire
horizon? What were we doing when we unchained this
earth from its sun? Whither is it moving now? Whither
are we moving? Away from all suns? Are we not
plunging continually? Backward, sideward, forward, in
all directions? Is there any up or down? Are we not
straying as through an infinite nothing? Do we not feel
the breath of empty space? Has it not become colder?
Is not night continually closing in on us?...What was
holiest and most powerful of all that the world has
owned has bled to death under our knives: who will
wipe this blood of us?...'

Here the madman fell silent and looked again at his
listeners; and they, too, were silent and stared at him in
astonishment. At last he threw his lantern on the
ground, and broke it and went out. 'I come too early,'
he said then; 'my time is not yet. This tremendous
event is still on its way... – it has not yet reached the
ears of man. Lightning and thunder require time,
the light of the stars requires time, deeds, though done,
still require time to be seen and heard. This deed is still
more distant from them than the most distant stars –
and yet they have done it themselves.' It has been related
further that on that same day the madman forced his
way into several churches and there struck up his
requiem aeternam deo. Led out and called to account,
he is said to have replied every time, 'What after all
are these churches now if they are not the tombs and
sepulchers of God?'[14]

The parable is an extraordinarily rich tapestry of ideas. Kaufmann has argued that to assume Nietzsche was an atheist because of this parable is to miss its central point. Nietzsche was clearly anti-Christian and the Christian conception of God. But an attack on the Christian God is not the aim of the parable. Nietzsche proclaimed a pessimistic philosophy of nihilism in an age which celebrated the great achievements of humanity. Nietzsche is the madman of the parable and he has come too soon. Humanity is not worried by the death of God, it is a joke. Humanity feels itself equipped to rearrange the cosmos. So the torrent of questions is greeted with stunned silence. All that is left is to appeal to the Christians who must surely be worried that their God has died.

Before the madman realizes that he has come too soon he bombards the traders and shoppers with questions. This is the heart of the parable. What will they do now they no longer have God to support an ethical and moral framework? What values can survive the removal of God? Nietzsche wanted to know how humanity could be ethical if the only end of humanity was itself. The death of God meant that the value of humanity has been diminished. In Kaufmann's words, 'the death of God threatened human life with a complete loss of all significance'.[15]

I have consistently argued that we are not at Nietzsche's nightmare point yet; nor of course will we inevitably go there. In the meantime, what we can see is that just as belief in God remains, so does ethics. The ongoing life of God results in a continuation of a concern with values and morals. Following Nietzsche's analysis, whilst God lives on so will our ability to debate and discuss what constitutes the good life. In other words, the West is an ethics society, a concept we will go on to explore in the next chapter.

The main purpose of this chapter has been to show how the Victorian period was a time of exceptionally high church attendance and support. The nineteenth century was a major peak in the wave-like history of Christianity. The reason for this was the enormous effort at evangelization undertaken by

the Church. I have focused on two prominent tools of evangelization, the home visit and the tract. These were part of a
wider culture which brought people into church in great
numbers. Alongside the dominance of evangelical Christian
culture, we have seen that organized secularism failed to gain
a significant foothold in Western culture. The secular societies
were a minor part of social life, as they remain to this
day. Intellectual ideas have had a more substantial impact on
society. But what they reveal is the remarkable ability of
Christianity to adopt and transform almost any set of ideas or
beliefs. Finally, we have looked at Nietzsche's premature
announcement of the death of God. I have argued that
Nietzsche was correct in one respect, namely that belief in
God runs in conjunction with a concern for ethics. A society
that believes in God has ethical questions at its centre. This is
the condition of Western secular society, as explored in the
final chapter.

Chapter Nine

The Ethics Society

The purpose of this book is to describe the religious identity of Western society. Through my survey of certain points in Christian history, I am reinterpreting what it means to call the West secular. The aim of this chapter is to pull together the analysis and discussion of the previous chapters, so that we end up with a coherent description of Western secular society. The first stage is to summarize my conclusions so far. This will entail revisiting the four key ideas which were outlined in Chapter One. I shall then examine two issues in detail. The first is to ask what it means to talk about liberalism as a Christian way of undertaking ethics. Are we saying merely that liberalism has its origins in Christianity or are we saying that liberal ethics in some way illustrates an ongoing Christian reality? It will be my contention that we need to think of liberalism as a contemporary Christian expression of ethical life. I shall then go on to look at an important criticism of the idea that liberalism and Christianity should be so closely integrated. There are significant and influential theologians who argue that the Church is a corrective to Western liberal society. Liberalism amounts to a self-interested and alienated individualism which fails to offer people a solid notion of what constitutes the common good. By contrast, the Church is a community which nurtures people in the skills and virtues needed to live the moral life. If this criticism is accurate then the integration of Christianity and liberalism I am exploring would not be possible. So these arguments must be examined carefully. Then in the final section of the chapter I shall bring together the discussion by offering a summary of the religious identity of Western secular society. The title offered for my description of the West is the ethics society.

I began the book with four propositions. It is worth recapping on these propositions to remind ourselves of the point we have so far reached. The first was that Christianity has a history of adopting and transforming indigenous religious cultures. This is especially true when these cultures are so strongly imbedded within local populations that they resist being swept away by the Church. This process of adoption and transformation Anton Wessels calls ongoing inculturation. The consequence of inculturation is that Christianity has a fluid identity. Christianity is in a state of regular change and renewal. An important illustration of the process is the celebration of Easter. In some Northern European countries this has obvious parallels with the festival of the goddess Ostara. The festival celebrations were during springtime and focused on rebirth, fertility and new life. We can assume that as Christianity spread to these countries it was unable to remove the strong local attachment to the goddess. So it adopted the beliefs linked with the goddess' cult and turned them into Christian beliefs. This process will have had the reciprocal effect of altering Christian beliefs. As the process of inculturation is a permanent feature of Christianity, so its identity is constantly in a state of change. One resulting question for the Church is where and how does this inculturation occur today? My answer is that one place to look is the development of liberal ideology in the West.

I then argued that an investigation of the Middle Ages revealed similarities in Christian belief and practice between the medieval period and our own age. The focus of the study was on popular belief. I found that ordinary people were capable of constructing a set of beliefs which functioned effectively in their lives. In particular, Christianity had a technological function which afforded the hope of medical cures as well as protection from dangerous natural phenomena. So previously blessed candles were lit and placed in windows during thunderstorms; sailors bent coins when caught in storms; and the sick travelled some distance for cures at the shrines of saints. Alongside this, another feature of medieval religion was that many exercised their faith vicariously. They desired other people to be active, engaged Christians on their behalf. They wanted to see a pure, holy Church, but they did not expect or wish to be involved themselves. Saints were the most important group of Christians to whom ordinary people could turn for support. Their good works were the key to divine protection and approval and so their favour needed to be courted. The indulgences system was founded on the excessive holiness of the saints. But this was not the only way in which religion worked vicariously. Some might also pay others to make pilgrimages on their behalf. This was often requested in wills as it was important prior to the moment of divine judgment to have fulfilled all one's holy obligations. I also noted that medieval people were committed to Christian ethics. The 'Seven Works of Mercy' illustrate the importance of ethics. There was a general and significant concern for the poorest people in society. This again could have been functional in that it was seen as a necessary aspect of the requirements of salvation. Or it could have been motivated by a genuine feeling for the suffering of poor people.

My third proposition looked at the events of the Enlightenment. What emerged at the Enlightenment was a scientific mentality. This became the new technology of Western society, replacing Christianity. This scientific mentality remains to the present day. Newton is credited with making the major contribution to this new way of understanding the world. It is an empirical methodology based on mathematics, observation and experiment. It overthrew the Cartesian system which had previously dominated science. Voltaire was instrumental in promoting Newton's fame through the popularizing of his work. The development of a scientific mentality did not lead to the end of belief in God. Despite the attacks on the Church by Voltaire and others, belief in God did not and has not disappeared. This means most people have a dual mentality. The scientific mentality coexists with an ongoing belief in God. Newton himself led the way. What we have after the Enlightenment, despite strong anti-clericalism, especially in countries such as France, is a dual mentality which is both scientific and also professes some form of theism.

I then examined some conclusions from political theorists who have investigated the historical origins of liberal theory. It was argued that liberalism stems from and is an expression of Christianity. The individualism at the heart of liberalism developed from the Christian idea that we are all children of God. A question remains as to whether this Christian analysis of liberalism is just an historic legacy or whether it has an ongoing contemporary reality. I shall discuss this later in the chapter. The conclusion reached now is that the liberal tradition only makes sense because of its Christian identity.

The fourth and final proposition is that the Victorian era was a time of exceptionally high levels of Christian belief and practice. This was the result of an enormous effort at evangelization by nineteenth-century voluntary societies. They employed a systematic programme of home visiting. This entailed dividing up streets, knocking on doors and recording what was found, be it Christian welcome or heathen rejection. The scheme of home visiting was combined with a major effort to publish Christian literature. A vast number of short tracts were distributed. They contained exhortations to moral living and biblical extracts. Magazines were also published with stories of how the immoral suffered bad ends, whilst the good were rewarded. Obituaries fulfilled the same purpose as the praises of a good woman were sung. The effect of both the visiting and the publication and distribution of so much literature was the Christianization of the nation. It resulted in large numbers of people attending church. It also led to a dominant Christian culture. This had a particular focus on the religious and cultural identity of women. The image of the good woman was one of cleanliness, thrift, sober living and piety. With the collapse of this image in the 1960s, churchgoing levels declined rapidly.

Any period of Christian history which followed such a comprehensive effort at Christianization was bound to appear to be in decline. However, in fact what we are witnessing today may just be a reversion to more normal levels of Church allegiance and support. Christian belief and practice is now at a level comparable with the medieval period if we allow for local factors. These local factors could include the important social and community role played by some churches in the Middle Ages. This would have led to higher levels of attendance. Or it might have meant an absentee priest or a community without a local church building, and therefore lower levels of attendance than a contemporary church with an active minister. The 'culture wars' in the USA are another example of local factors affecting the prominence of Christian culture and, at the very least, reported numbers of churchgoers. But given the exceptions which take into account these local circumstances, our religious life is similar to the medieval period and considerably different from the Victorian age.

This has led me to describe Christian history as a succession of peaks and troughs. It is something akin to a wave-like history rather than a linear rise or decline. Professor David Martin writes in similar terms in his recent book on secularization.[1] He argues that secularization is not a once and for all 'unilateral process'. Instead, it is better to think 'in terms of successive Christianizations followed or accompanied by recoils'. There were four key moments in Christian history. Martin argues as follows:

> I identify, first, a Catholic Christianization in two versions: the conversion of monarchs (and so of peoples), and the conversion of the urban masses by

the friars. I then identify a Protestant Christianization in two versions: one seeking to extend the monasticism to all Christian people but effectively corralling them in the nation, and the other realized in the creation of evangelical and Pietist subcultures. This last collapsed quite recently so we are immediately in its wake.[2]

The rite of baptism illustrates the point. At the key points in Christian history, baptism was an initiation into membership of different groupings. So there might be baptism as a right for all and into membership of Christendom, or there might be baptism into the nation or baptism into a denominational subculture. Martin's history of peaks and troughs highlights alternate historical points from our own analysis. This is because of our focus on popular belief and our concentration on the situation in the West, illustrated by religious belief and practice in the UK. But the principle of analysing the historic movement of Christianity in terms of peaks and troughs is the same.

I noted that Friedrich Nietzsche had drawn an explicit link between belief in God and ethical values. The parable of the madman proclaiming the death of God was used by Nietzsche to make his point. If we remove belief in God then we lose the capacity to make ethical judgments. Belief in God sustains the principles and values which underpin society.

Nietzsche's point agrees with my analysis so far. Together with the conclusions from other chapters, it leads us to describe Western society as the ethics society. In this chapter I shall go on to describe what I mean by an ethics society in more detail. In summary, and quite straightforwardly, what I am arguing is that Western society is an ethics society because it is fundamentally preoccupied with ethical questions. The particular manifestation of this preoccupation at the moment is the concern that liberal theory, and its manifestation in Western polity, has led to relativism. That is, liberalism has lost, or never had, an anchoring in a sense of what constitutes good behaviour and now gives permission for individuals to do whatever they think best. Some Christians condemn liberal society for its lack of moral direction and want to call it back to a notion of the common good. They wish to define an idea of what constitutes good living, which should then shape contemporary society through the example of the Church. This is an attempt to correct the anti-Christian direction taken by important liberals. But if liberalism itself is a manifestation of Christianity then this becomes an internal debate about the process of inculturation with liberalism. It is a theological dispute, albeit one from which doctrinal concerns are absent.

The central question is about the process of inculturation between Christianity and liberalism. Historical analysis of how Christianity moves between different societies and cultures leads to the argument that both these positions are expressions of different types of inculturation. One group is heavily inculturated with liberalism. The other rejects liberal ideology, sometimes despite its protestations to the contrary. The latter group inculturates with anti-liberal theory and polity, most commonly ideas found within pre-modern forms of Christianity. In other words, the choice within the ethics society is what value should be placed on liberal values and norms. I shall argue that a defining characteristic of Western secular society is the popular support for liberal ethics. This is related to belief in God and an expression of Christian identity.

In order to examine the identity of the ethics society, I shall explore two issues. First, I will investigate the already highlighted question of whether Western society's liberalism is a product of an historic Christian legacy or a contemporary expression of Christianity. This is necessary if I am to argue that Christianity has a modern, and inculturated, identity as liberal ethics. Second, I discuss the arguments of those who disagree with my analysis. In particular, I look at those who believe there is an important distinction to be made between Christianity and liberal society.

Liberalism and Christian Ethics

What do I mean when I argue that liberal theory is Christian? Is it simply saying that the early liberal theorists were Christians and therefore liberalism grew out of a Christian context? Or is it an attempt to say more than this? Should we think of liberalism as a form or expression of Christianity? I shall argue that liberalism is the ethical guidance by which most people in the West give substance to their belief in God. People believe in God and seek to be good. Liberalism is the way they achieve the second of these aims.

To begin with, it should be noted that there is a danger that a discussion of the relationship between liberalism and Christianity could get bogged down in ever more detailed definitions. Such a path would not serve the purposes of the book, namely understanding the religious and cultural identity of the West. It is better to proceed by removing any possible confusions and then seeing what can be added to the analysis. The first point to be made is that I am not suggesting that all advocates of liberal theory are recognizably Christian. You do not have to be a Church member, profess a belief in God or be implicitly Christian to be a liberal. It is possible to be liberal and an atheist. If a liberal theorist were atheist then this does not detract from my argument.

Second, not all Christians are liberal. It is possible to be a Christian and committed to authoritarian forms of government and the removal of individual human rights. The Church of England has important exemptions from UK employment legislation as an acknowledgement that its position in regard to a liberal polity is exceptional. The examples from history of an anti-liberal and Christian combination are legion. More than this, the question of whether all Christians are liberals or all liberals are Christians is not one I am trying to address. It does not pertain directly to my argument.

The reasons such qualifications are necessary is that it is very easy to cause offence by appropriating individuals for an identity they wish to reject. However, my aim is not to reach conclusions about the thought of a few individuals, mainly in the academy. Their work is important and has helped in developing my analysis; but it is not the purpose of the book to highlight some mistake made by those who do not describe themselves as Christian or liberal. What I am seeking to do is to describe the culture which shapes the perspective of the majority. It is the religious identity of the 70 per cent or so who believe in God, but are not formally attached to a church, that I seek to understand and describe. The argument is that the culture which shapes the views of these people can be called Christian. What this entails is changing the definition of what constitutes Christian belief and practice.

The attempt to redefine the boundaries of Christian belief by lowering the threshold goes against recent Church practice. There has been a trend towards setting the standard of Christian identity ever higher. David Martin notes that after the end of Christendom: 'Christians have raised the bar about what it means to be Christian, and so inhibited the take-up.'[3] People have been placed into the secular category because they do not attain the 'virtuoso performance' of the elite. The apathetic middle ground, between committed Christian devotion and militant atheism, has been excluded from the Church. These people are thought of as secular. Evangelicals have done this by stressing the need for genuine experience and a change of life. Catholics have done it by emphasizing the importance of personal devotion and commitment to the Eucharist. This inevitably makes any attempt at re-Christianization all the more difficult. But we could set about shifting the bar. If the qualification for Christian identity was a commitment to the contemporary expression of Christian ethics through liberalism, then many more people would belong. The question is whether we have grounds for describing liberal ethics as Christian and as prevalent in Western society?

One of the difficulties with analysing the prevalence of liberal Christian ethics is that it so pervades our culture that we hardly notice its presence. Liberalism has a taken-for-granted status which means we can miss the enormous influence it has on our ethical thinking. It is only when we make statements which are not informed by these principles and values that their prevalence becomes apparent.[4] Fortunately, the previously mentioned work by John Gray, *Straw Dogs*, undertakes such a task.[5] If we examine his ideas we get a sense of how influential liberal ethics are.

Gray argues that as a result of Darwin's theory of evolution, we should think of human beings as animals like any other. Darwin has argued, successfully for Gray, that what controls and directs human life is the desire for evolutionary success. In this, humans are just like other animals. The notion that humanity has any sort of special status is a pre-Darwinian myth. The special status of human beings is a Christian doctrine which has been undone by Darwinism.[6] This has a whole series of implications. It is when we examine the implications that we see what a non-liberal society might look like. Gray presents a form of evolutionary nihilism as an alternative to liberalism.

A major tenet of evolutionary nihilism is the idea that the search for truth is a luxury. It serves to protect humanity from the despair that comes from nihilism. It is a strategy which shields human beings from knowing there is no purpose to life beyond the survival of the species for as long as that fits the workings of the Earth. Human beings will abandon such luxuries in times of crisis. Then human aims are to protect their offspring, revenge themselves on their enemies and 'give vent' to their feelings. These are not flaws in humanity. They cannot be changed or improved by science or reason. They are characteristics. They are no more than the logical consequence of recognizing that humans are survival machines.[7]

A second key notion is that morality is a human myth derived from the superstitions of Judaism and Christianity. Again in times of crisis, human beings will not be moral; they will seek to survive. Gray tells the story of Roman Frister to illustrate the point.[8] Frister was raped by a German guard in a Nazi concentration camp. The guard then stole Frister's cap because he knew that if a prisoner appeared on parade without a cap then they would be shot. This would ensure the crime went unreported. To survive, Frister stole another prisoner's cap. The second prisoner was shot on morning parade. Frister reports his feelings at the moment of execution as not being remorse, shame or guilt. It was delight at being alive, to have survived. Gray's point is that what we think of as morality is suspended in times of crisis. At such times, human nature reveals itself as lawless in the interests of survival.

Gray describes humans as natural killers. He states that 'Genocide is as human as prayer or art'. Humans are not uniquely murderous. Monkeys are violent. If they were equipped with human technology then they may well kill each other in as large a number as humans do. Gray states: 'Humans are weapon-making animals with an unquenchable fondness for killing'.[9] There is of course a lot of evidence of human murder and Gray lists this to support his point. It ranges from the Nazis to Stalin and Rwanda.

The last illustration we shall offer is Gray's discussion of the will. Starting with the philosopher Schopenhauer, Gray argues that there is no such thing as reason.[10] There is only human will, a will to exercise power and to dominate. We employ reason in the service of this will. The notion of reason helps us in our struggles to survive and prosper. But it is not autonomous and it does not lead to the truth. Our will is employed to ensure our evolutionary survival.

The point of listing these examples is not to begin a discussion about evolutionary nihilism. There are of course many philosophers and theologians who would want to argue that Gray misses much that is morally excellent about humanity. They would want to cite illustrations of human generosity and selflessness from throughout history, including of course from the Holocaust. There are also many people who would find Gray's analysis appalling. But our purpose is not to decide whether Gray is correct; rather, it is to show the extent to which liberal values underpin the norms of Western social life. In contemporary Western society, most people believe there is an ethical code which shapes human behaviour. Moral values are real and important, not a myth or superstition to be dismissed in the interests of survival. They believe society can progress and that such progression is achieved through education and science. The idea of personal and social progression gives meaning to life. They believe human beings are individuals who should take responsibility for their actions. Human actions should be weighed against a moral code. People are not just another species of animal. This moral code allows people to live together in society. And society is itself an illustration of the social nature of humanity. We do not choose to live alone, engaged only in self-interested action. We choose to live together and to help one another. Western society is proud of its compassion and generosity to its own members and people in other countries. This is not a textbook definition of liberalism. But the rejection of Gray, or his description as nihilist, shows how liberal ethics underpin the social and cultural values of Western society.

The significant point in our argument is that this cultural influence is contemporary. To describe humanity in the nihilist way Gray does is to invite widespread criticism. And this refusal to agree with Gray reveals the extent to which most people in the West are informed by the values and principles he wants to reject. What this means is that Christian ethics, as expressed in the values of liberal society, is more than an historical legacy. It is a real and active presence in Western society. The West has its contemporary life shaped by what are identifiably Christian ethical values.

There is one final point of clarification to be made in our discussion about the relationship between Christianity and the ethics of liberal society. It will have been noticed that I am talking about complex areas with a wide range of definitions and long histories. My discussions have been couched in very broad terms. This means a lot of the details of how liberalism evolved and is distinct from humanism have been ignored. There is a question about whether this is legitimate. It may not be sufficiently accurate or detailed enough to talk about liberalism and humanism and Western secular society in the way I have. In one sense this is a valid criticism. I have not provided evidence to suggest that the notion of freedom of speech or parliamentary democracy is a product of Christian theological thought. There is no direct link made, for example, between the right of association and a doctrine of human sinfulness. It is also true that I have conflated humanism with liberalism. Furthermore, I have talked about Western society as liberal when some argue that it has rejected some of the core features of a fully and properly functioning liberalism.

What I have done instead is write in very general terms about liberal society and liberal values and principles. Likewise, I have done the same for humanism and Christianity. The reason for this is that I am seeking to analyse and discuss the West's popular and general culture. This is not an examination of liberal theory in any of its specific forms. It is instead a narrative about a society which on the whole calls itself liberal. So my broad use of the terms reflect the concern to discuss society as a whole, reflected in what might be thought of as cultural norms. This is a dangerous business in that it will lead to very general impressions. However, its value is that it enables us to think in new and productive ways about Western society. The contention is that generalizations help this discussion.

In the first part of this chapter I have outlined the argument made so far in the book. I have then argued that Western society is influenced by Christian ethics through its acceptance of liberal norms and values. I illustrated the point negatively. That is, I looked at a philosophy which rejected dominant liberal values and principles. This philosophy was so far from what influences and dominates Western society's public discussions that it shows the ongoing importance of Christian liberal values. This point will be disputed by those who argue there is a major distinction between liberal society and the Church. In the next section of the chapter, I shall explore those contrasting views.

Let the Church be the Church

A major criticism of the integrated relationship between Christianity and liberalism that I am proposing comes from those who argue that there is a fundamental clash between the two sets of beliefs. They argue that the role of the Church, and this is its political role, is to stand as an alternative to the dominant liberal political order of Western society. What I am suggesting would prevent this oppositional role because of the way we have merged Christianity and liberal thought. The most influential example of this critical position is the US theologian Professor Stanley Hauerwas. I shall begin by exploring his critique of the Western liberal political order.[11]

The fundamental difference between liberal theory and Christianity, according to Hauerwas, is that Christianity has a notion of what constitutes the good in the moral or ethical life. Liberalism is seen as lacking a substantial description of primary ethical values. In fact, liberalism was developed as an ideology to cope with the plurality of different conceptions of political and religious truth. Liberalism is a method by which this diversity is managed in a society that wants to coexist without overt violent conflict. So liberalism is a set of procedures by which people in society can deal with the problem that they do not have a shared history.[12] It has no philosophical or ethical content beyond the resolution of conflict between self-interested groups and individuals. All that is required is that the individuals or groups consent to be subject to the rules by which the disagreements are resolved.

This puts the individual at the heart of liberal theory. This individual is a self-centred and self-interested being. This does not matter to liberalism as long as the individual will prioritize living alongside other equally self-interested individuals without violence. When interests clash, the self-centred individual must put conflict–resolution procedures above their own selfish concerns. This is what democracy achieves. It is a set of mechanisms for allowing the resolution of conflict without physical violence. Those who condemn democratic politics would argue that there is verbal and emotional violence in the discussions between opposing groups and that electoral triumph can be akin to victory in war. But the absence of bloodshed is a significant improvement on what went before. This of course does not mean liberal democracies cannot be violent to others; but their internal disputes are resolved in this type of peaceable manner.

Theologians who argue this point critique liberal theorists who attempt to build substantial concepts of what is ethical through procedural mechanisms. For example, Stanley Hauerwas is critical of John Rawls' attempt to construct a concept of justice through the employment of political procedures. What is missing is a full definition of what is good and moral. Rawls offers a sophisticated tool for discerning the nature of justice, known as the 'original position'. There is only space to describe this much discussed and developed mechanism very briefly. In essence, Rawls says that the way to decide what is just is to argue from the perspective that society should be organized so that all individuals and groups are treated fairly. The effects of economic and social advantage should be eliminated. Rawls asks us to imagine that we have to develop the principles by which society is justly ordered without any knowledge of our own social position. This is the original position. The expectation is that the political order developed in this way will not favour any individual or social group. What Hauerwas argues is that this demonstrates the flaws of liberal theory. It reveals how liberalism has a notion of the individual as self-interested and free-floating. That is an individual shorn of any historical location. If we are in Rawls' original position without knowledge of our social status, then we have no individuality. Such a non-historical individual cannot exist of course. It is a cipher. Furthermore, such an individual lacks the self-interested perspective that makes him or her different from other self-interested individuals. This means, and this is the paradox of the procedure according to Hauerwas, that the original position functions by eradicating the individual differences which first made it necessary. Hauerwas expresses the point well himself:

The recent emphasis on 'justice' in the elegant ethical
and political theory elaborated by John Rawls might be
taken to indicate that liberalism is capable of a
profounder sense of justice than I have described.
Without going into the detailed argument necessary to
criticize Rawls, his books stands as a testimony to the
moral limits of the liberal tradition. For the 'original
position' is a stark metaphor for the ahistorical
approach of liberal theory, as the self is alienated from
its history and simply left with its individual
preferences and prejudices. The 'justice' that results
from the bargaining game is but the guarantee that my
liberty to consume will be fairly limited within the
overall distributive shares. To be sure, some concern for
the 'most disadvantaged' is built into the system, but
not in a manner that qualifies my appropriate concern
for self-interest. Missing entirely from Rawls' position
is any suggestion that a theory of justice is ultimately
dependent on a view of the good; or that justice is as
much a category for individuals as for societies. The
question is not only how should the shares of any
society be distributed equitably, but what bounds
should individuals set for themselves if they are to be
just.[13]

Hauerwas goes on to state that Rawls has been forced, in the
interests of abolishing envy, into ensuring all desires are equal
if society is to be just. The irony is that to achieve social
justice between competing individuals, the very substance
of individuality must be abolished. The point being that without such differences individuals merge into a form of blank
collective. Hauerwas argues that not all desires should be
treated equally. Those individuals skilled in virtuous living
may well have far more just desires than those not so formed.

What is being discussed here is the nature of individualism
in liberal society. The question is whether the individual
is allowed to believe what they like and do what they want, as

long as it is within the confines of the liberal political order. The alternative to the ahistorical liberal individual is the community which knows what is true and thereby sets limits to what the individual may believe. A liberal individual may construct their own story. A community-based individual is shaped by the community's story.

What Hauerwas has in mind is the Church. The Church so educates and one might say indoctrinates people, if this can be a good thing, that their first instinct is to live ethically. Through the business of community living, prayer, worship, study, involvement in social projects and political campaigns, the outlook of people is fundamentally shaped. They naturally choose the moral path which is an expression of the Christianity which pervades their life. This means the Church's primary role in society is not to join in political campaigns and elections. Rather, the primary role of the Church is to be itself. It means the Church standing as an alternative community to, but within, the liberal political order. Only then can people be formed to live ethically in liberal society. At the heart of the Church's alternative identity is the knowledge that it has a true story about humanity. The Church has a saviour who limits the sovereignty of political and social movements. The Church embodies a notion of what constitutes moral good. This does not mean the Church should reject all social orders or withdraw from engagement with politics. Hauerwas is clear it should not. But it does mean that the Church's first duty is to be faithful to itself. This entails exhibiting a type of community life which is possible when it is trust and not fear which governs individual lives.[14]

There is much in Hauerwas' work that has been subject to intense discussion and criticism. It is not necessary for us to investigate all of these discussions.[15] But we can focus on one alternative to Hauerwas' story of liberalism. By looking at this alternative view, we shall get closer to the heart of the argument. The major proponent of the alternative view is Professor Jeffrey Stout.[16] He argues that there is more to democracy than a mere set of procedures by which otherwise

self-interested individuals seek to coexist. There is a democratic tradition and a set of virtues which shape the democrat's
life. What is interesting about Stout's analysis of the democratic tradition is that he gives the procedural convenience of
liberalism an ethical substance. It is to this I now turn.

Stout recognizes that some people in liberal societies will
hold religious views which will influence significantly the
contribution they wish to make to public debates.[17] This is
especially true of the US political context from which he
writes. But these religious people in liberal society recognize
quite pragmatically that their religious motivations and justi-
fications are not shared by everyone else. If they are very
pragmatic, they may calculate that their religious views are
not shared by a sufficient majority of other people to win
whatever discussion is underway. So they present their views
in ways which can be agreed with by people who do not share
their religious perspective. Thereby, they can achieve a working political alliance. What this means is that the absence of
religious language from Western liberal democratic discussion
is a practical means of coping with pluralism.

At this point, Stout might seem to be being procedural in his
explanation of liberal democracy. But the next point refutes
such an analysis. Stout argues that liberal democracy in the
USA has a history and a tradition. The value of the tradition is
that it can equip citizens with the skills and resources needed
to protect and enhance liberal democracy. There are skills to be
utilized when living in a democratic society. They are: 'certain
habits of reasoning, certain attitudes toward deference and
authority in political discussion, and love for certain goods and
virtues, as well as a disposition to respond to certain types of
actions, events, or persons with admiration, pity, or horror.'[18]
What threatens liberal democracy is not an empty individualism, that is an individualism concerned only with people's selfish interests, but the demise of the habits and practices needed
to be democratic. Stout's criticism against those who attack liberalism is that, if they are influential like Hauerwas, then they
undermine the resilience of the democratic tradition.

What this means is that the individual of the liberal tradition is not a cipher. The liberal individual, who lives in democratic society, is part of a tradition. Furthermore, they are offered certain habits and skills. Hence the liberal individual can be judged as living well or badly under a democratic order and a society may do more or less to be democratic. In this sense, democracy is a liberal moral good.

At the heart of the discussion is the question of a forming tradition. This is the issue which Stout's analysis raises. For Hauerwas, liberalism creates people who have to deny their individuality to be able to have a notion of justice. For Stout, liberalism can lead to skilled democratic practitioners. I have argued that the liberal tradition is an ongoing expression of Christianity, so people influenced by liberalism are in some current form behaving in a Christian manner. Liberalism has substance because it is a contemporary expression of Christianity. Those formed in a liberal political order can be skilled Christian practitioners. The issue is who has a correct understanding of the relationship between Christianity and liberalism.

It might be supposed that the way to address this question is to examine in detail the history of liberalism. This is pos-sible; however, the problem with such an approach is one of perspective. There is such a vast amount of evidence, of differing types, that historians and political theorists could reach competing conclusions. A case either for or against the close connection of liberalism and Christianity could be made from the sources available. There are examples of liberal theorists who seem fully indebted to Christianity, and then there are those who seem to reject fully any Christian influence. Locke and Kant are examples of the first perspective, whilst Mill would be a good illustration of the second. What this means is that it is more profitable to note that how we analyse the relationship stems from our view of Western liberal society. It depends on whether we think contemporary Western society, dominated as it is by liberal ideals, is also Christian. There are those, like Hauerwas, who have clearly rejected the Christian basis of liberalism. By contrast, I have maintained that Western society displays signs of being significantly shaped by Christian values. My final task is to give some reasons for this view.

The Good Liberal Society

My main contention has been that Western secular society should be thought of as the ethics society. As such, it is a society primarily concerned with ethical issues, and the concern for ethics is discernibly Christian, but I want to argue more than this. Many of the conclusions reached by Western liberal and secular society are recognizably Christian. By this I mean that the situation of marginalized and excluded people cannot be ignored by social and political leaders. This is not an easy case to argue. There is a dilemma of how to speak well of a society which knows itself to be failing. It would in many ways be better not to have to make the case. But the strength of the criticisms made by those who regard liberal society as anti-Christian mean the attempt is necessary. So it is necessary to take the risk of praising that which could be far better. This is the dilemma of the ethics society. It is not meant to lead to political complacency; quite the opposite. The Western liberal political order is capable of good, as well as bad, and so deserves our serious attention.

What we see in Western society is the prominence of an ethical concern in virtually all areas of life. Science produces ethical problems. These arise in medical science, such as the high-profile issues of abortion, stem cell research, human cloning and euthanasia. Western society has not found a shared means of agreeing its stance on these issues, beyond the legal minimums. But it does regard them as of central importance. Science has also identified an ethical problem with regard to the environment. Scientists have analysed the problems of global warming and the depletion of the ozone layer. They have also suggested the means by which humans might change their behaviour to reduce these problems. Again ,we are not suggesting that these problems have been resolved. What we are saying is that it is a feature of Western society that these issues are of shared public ethical concern.

We can also see in social and political policy a recognition that people shaped by Western culture will not allow the poorest and the oppressed to be deliberately excluded. For example, the question of the most appropriate form of social welfare is a permanent political topic. There are of course differences in priorities. Western Europe is well known for spending greater proportions of public money on state welfare systems than the USA. Many argue that more should be spent and that taxes should be higher. But in no country in the West is it publicly agreed that the plight of the poorest or the sick should not be a concern. Elections cannot be won this way. Often the language of rights will apply as equally to those who are oppressed in society as it will to those who are powerful and wealthy. When relationships break up, the fate of children is seen as paramount.

The West is also prepared to undertake major social reforms because of its ethical commitment to individual rights. So women have an economic, social and political status in contemporary society rarely enjoyed previously in Western social history. The same can be said of Black and Asian people and those in same-sex relationships. The rights language extends to those outside of Western society. There is a real sense that a shared human bond means that when people die of curable diseases or starvation or acts of genocide, then Western citizens expect action from their political leaders. Furthermore, such action is frequently forthcoming because the political leaders know the pressure is real.

At this point it is necessary to stop before my argument is dismissed as naive nonsense. It is rare to celebrate the achievements of Western society. The norm is to criticize the ordering of the West because of its many faults. Racism is still endemic in society. Women are often excluded from the higher echelons of the workplace. Those in same-sex relationships, as well as women and Black and Asian people, experience brutal, unprovoked violence. The functioning of the democratic polity is hugely dependent on wealth, power and media influence. The West is all too willing to engage in war. I am not denying these painful truths. The argument is not that the West is an ideal, far from it. Nor at this stage can the position of the author be ignored. It is all too easy to celebrate a society in which a high level of contentment has been achieved. Furthermore, it is true that a radical re-ordering of society will benefit many of those who are excluded now. So I do not believe this is the best of all possible worlds. I am not suggesting we all become Leibniz's disciples. But if we decide to end the liberal polity or replace liberalism with an anti-liberal ideology, or theology, then we must be aware of what we will lose. The end of liberal society will only come with a major social cost.

The difficulty experienced here comes from recognizing the tension at the heart of the ethics society. What we are trying to say is that our society is ethical, it has an essential concern for the nature of what constitutes moral good, but it equally has the capacity radically to exclude people from that good. It is a society that can construct itself so that it both exists in a manner preoccupied with being generous to those who are oppressed, whilst also oppressing these people. Does this make it Christian? Of course, it by no means matches the Christian ideal. But if we compare it with the evolutionary nihilism of Gray then it does. Western society does not believe or celebrate the description of humans as killing machines. It does not regard genetic survival as its greatest achievement. It does not act as though morality is a myth or superstition. It may be deceiving itself in these matters, but that is not its culture. The West's ethical discussions and achievements mean it is accurate to describe it as a culture living with a Christian conception of the moral good.

Conclusion

We are now in a position to summarize the religious and cultural identity of Western secular society. The people who live in contemporary Western secular society have a dual mentality. They are convinced of the functional superiority of the scientific method for resolving technological problems. This forms their commitment to science. But people realize that the scientific methodology cannot address ethical issues. What science allows for is unlimited technological advance. But it has no inbuilt means of deciding that some advances are good and some are wrong. So they fall back on their traditional means of making ethical decisions, namely Christianity.

One of the odd features of secular society is that a majority within it believe in God. What we have been arguing is that this expression of belief is a serious proposition. Christian culture has changed since the Victorian era. It is less dominant and fewer people now attend church in almost all parts of the West. But the Victorian period was exceptional for its high levels of Church allegiance. What has happened is that this fall-off has been described as a decline in Christianity. Against this, I have argued that it is more properly seen as a reversion to more normal levels of religious belief and practice. What is more likely is that Christianity is adapting and changing to the new conditions of post-Victorian Christianity. This new Christian shape has certain distinctive features. People tend to be vicarious in the exercise of their faith. The extent of their Christian knowledge depends on what their particular needs are. And people continue to rely on belief in God and a Christian presence to motivate and inspire their pervasive concern for ethics. These features combine to make up what we have called the ethics society. This is the dominant religious and cultural identity of Western secular society.

Notes

Chapter One – Western Secularism

1   National Statistics Online: http://www.statistics.gov.uk.
2   Halman, Loek, *The European Values Study: A Third Wave* (Le Tilburg, 2001), pp.81, 86.
3   Davie, Grace, *Religion in Britain since 1945* (Oxford, 1994).
4   Bruce, Steve, *Religion in the Modern World: From Cathedrals to Cults* (Oxford, 1996), p.38.
5   Davie, Grace, *Europe: The Exceptional Case* (London, 2002).
6   Davie notes that 57 per cent of the population in Ireland attend church once a week, a figure that drops to 14 per cent in Britain and only 4 per cent in Sweden. Davie: *Europe: The Exceptional Case*, p.6.
7   Halman: *The European Values Study*, p.81.
8   Gray, John, *Enlightenment's Wake: Politics and Culture at the Close of the Modern Age* (London, 1995); Siedentop, Larry, *Democracy in Europe* (London, 2000).
9   Bruce: *Religion in the Modern World*, p.30.

Chapter Two – Science: The New Technology

1   Russell, Bertrand, *History of Western Philosophy* (London, [1946] 1996), pp.68–9.

2   The last sentence paraphrases the American Quaker Rufus Jones. Interestingly, the churches have been as concerned about secularism as secular organizations. The Jerusalem Meeting of the International Missionary Council, a major international event in the Church's history, devoted a lot of attention to the subject of secularism. Much of what follows has been drawn from their work and in particular the address of Jones. Jones, Rufus, 'Secular civilization and the Christian task', in *The Christian Life and Message in Relation to Non-Christian Systems. Report of the Jerusalem Meeting of the International Missionary Council, 24 March to 8 April 1928*, Vol. 1 (London, 1928), pp.284–338.
3   Jones: 'Secular civilization and the Christian task', p.292.
4   Jones: 'Secular civilization and the Christian task', p.296.
5   Jacoby: *Freethinkers. A History of American Secularism* (New York, 2004). For details about Ingersoll see, especially, pp.157–85.
6   Jacoby: *Freethinkers. A History of American Secularism*, p.173.
7   See, for example, Dawkins, Richard, *God's gift to Kansas*, and, authored with Harries, Richard, then Bishop of Oxford, *Creationism is Bad Science and Bad Theology*, both available at the British Humanist Association website http://www.humanism.org.uk. The creationist view is well represented on the website of the Institute for Creation Research http://www.icr.org.
8   Tamimi, Azzam, 'The origins of Arab secularism', in J. Esposito and A. Tamimi (eds), *Islam and Secularism in the Middle East* (London, 2000), especially pp.13–16.
9   Gay, Peter, *Freud. A Life for our Time* (New York, 1988).
10   Freud, Sigmund, 'The future of an illusion', in *The Standard Edition of the Complete Psychological Works of Sigmund Freud*, Vol. XXI (1927–31), trans: Strachey, James (London, [1927] 1964), p.55.
11   Freud: 'The future of an illusion', p.16.
12   Freud: 'The future of an illusion', p.17.
13   Freud: 'The future of an illusion', p.18.
14   Freud: 'The future of an illusion', p.19.
15   Cited in Gay, Peter, *Freud. A Life for our Time*, p.524.
16   Freud: 'The future of an illusion', p.23.
17   Brown, Peter, *Augustine of Hippo. A Biography* (Berkeley, [1967] 2000), p.30.

Chapter Three – Secularism and Social History

1   For the work of Berger and Wilson see, especially, Berger, Peter, *The Social Reality of Religion* (Harmondsworth, 1972); and Wilson, Bryan, *Religion in Secular Society* (London, 1966).

2   Bruce, Steve, 'The demise of Christianity in Britain', in G. Davie, P. Heelas and L. Woodhead (eds), *Predicting Religion. Christian, Secular and Alternative Futures* (Ashgate, 2003), p.62.

3   See question 6C of Halman, Loek, *The European Values Study: A Third Wave. Source book of the 1999/2000 European Values Study surveys* (Le Tilburg, 2001), p.35.

4   Steve Bruce provides a useful summary of the data in his chapter in Davie, Heelas, and Woodhead: *Predicting Religion. Christian, Secular and Alternative Futures*, pp.54–7.

5   Bruce, Steve, *Religion in the Modern World. From Cathedrals to Cults* (Oxford, 1996), pp.39–52.

6   Bruce: *Religion in the Modern World*, p.45.

7   Bruce: *Religion in the Modern World*, p.52.

8   Davie, Grace, *Europe: The Exceptional Case. Parameters of Faith in the Modern World* (London, 2002), p.7.

9   Davie, Grace, *Religion in Britain Since 1945* (Oxford, 1994), especially Chapter Six.

10 Bruce: *Religion in the Modern World*, p.57.

11 See McLeod, Hugh, *Secularisation in Western Europe, 1848–1914* (New York, 2002), p.272; and Morris, Jeremy, 'The strange death of Christian Britain: Another look at the secularization debate', *The Historical Journal* 46/4 (2003). The works referred to are: Williams, Sarah, *Religious Belief and Popular Culture in Southwark, c. 1880–1939* (Oxford, 1999); Sykes, Richard, *Popular Religion in Dudley and the Gornals, c. 1914–1965* (unpublished University of Wolverhampton PhD thesis, 1999).

12 Cited in Morris: 'The strange death of Christian Britain', p.967.

13 Davie, Grace, *Religion in Modern Europe. A Memory Mutates* (Oxford, 2000).

14 See Davie's book of that title: Davie: *Europe: The Exceptional Case.*

15 Davie: *Europe: The Exceptional Case*, p.28.

16 Bruce: *Religion in the Modern World*, p.96.

17 Brown, Callum, *The Death of Christian Britain. Understanding Secularism 1800–2000* (London, 2001).

18 Brown: *The Death of Christian Britain*, p.162.

19 Brown: *The Death of Christian Britain*, p.170.

20 Brown: *The Death of Christian Britain*, p.172.

Chapter Four – The Reinvention of Christianity by Ordinary People

1   Kuhn, Thomas, *The Structure of Scientific Revolutions*, 2nd edn (Chicago, 1970); Wessels, Anton, *Europe: Was it Ever Really Christian?* (London, 1994).

2 Küng, Hans, 'Paradigm change in theology: A proposal for discussion', in H. Küng and D. Tracy, *Paradigm Change in Theology. A Symposium for the Future*, trans: Margaret Köhl (Edinburgh, 1989), p.7.

3 Bosch, David, *Transforming Mission. Paradigm Shifts in Theology of Mission* (Maryknoll, New York, 1991), pp.181–2. Küng and Bosch are indebted to the work by Thomas Kuhn as Bosch notes, pp.183–4.

4 Bosch: *Transforming Mission*, Chapter Six, pp.190–213.

5 Bosch: *Transforming Mission*, p.190.

6 Malherbe, Abraham, *Moral Exhortation. A Greco-Roman Sourcebook* (Philadelphia, 1986); Bosch: *Transforming Mission*, p.194.

7 Bosch: *Transforming Mission*, pp.206, 211.

8 Bosch: *Transforming Mission*, pp.190–1.

9 Bosch: *Transforming Mission*, p.211.

10 Küng: 'Paradigm change in theology: A proposal for discussion', p.30.

11 Wessels, Anton, *Europe: Was it Ever Really Christian?* (London, 1994), p.3.

12 Wessels: *Europe*, p.4.

13 Wessels: *Europe*, p.13.

14 Wessels: *Europe*, p.10.

15 Wessels: *Europe*, p.12. See Bede, *Ecclesiastical History of the English Nation* (London, 1910), Vol. II, p.11.

16 Wessels: *Europe*, pp.34–5.

17 Wessels: *Europe*, pp.35–6.

18 Wessels: *Europe*, p.36.

19 Wessels: *Europe*, p.41.

20 Wessels: *Europe*, p.42.

21 Wessels: *Europe*, p.44.

22 Wessels: *Europe*, p.154.

23 Wessels: *Europe*, p.154.

24 Wessels: *Europe*, p.166.

25 Crossan, John D., *The Historical Jesus. The Life of a Mediterranean Jewish Peasant* (Edinburgh, 1991), p.xxvii.

26 Crossan: *The Historical Jesus*, pp.xxvii–xxviii.

27 Nineham, Dennis, *Christianity Mediaeval and Modern* (London, 1993).

28 Newbigin wrote a number of small works exploring this theme. His major book, however, is: Newbigin, Lesslie, *The Gospel in a Pluralist Society* (London, 1989).

Chapter Five – Churchgoing and Pilgrimage in the Middle Ages

1 Duffy, Eamon, *The Stripping of the Altars. Traditional Religion in England 1400–1580*, 2nd edn (New Haven, 2005).

2   The section that follows is dependent upon Southern, *Western Society in the Middle Ages*, Chapter Two, pp.24–52.
3   Duffy: *The Stripping of the Altars*, pp.3–4.
4   For example: Gill, Robin, *The Empty Church Revisited* (Aldershot, 2003).
5   Brooke, Rosalind and Brooke, Christopher, *Popular Religion in the Middle Ages. Western Europe 1000–1300* (London, 1984).
6   Thomas, Keith, *Religion and the Decline of Magic. Studies in Popular Beliefs in Sixteenth and Seventeenth England* (London, 1973), especially Chapter One, pp.3–24.
7   Shinners, John (ed), *Medieval Popular Religion 1000–1500. A Reader* (Ontario, 1997), p.162.
8   Duffy: *The Stripping of the Altars*, p.11.
9   Duffy: *The Stripping of the Altars*, p.112.
10   Duffy: *The Stripping of the Altars*, p.93.
11   Hamilton, Bernard, *Religion in the Medieval West*, 2nd edn (London, 2003), p.89.
12   Thomas: *Religion and the Decline of Magic*, p.191.
13   Duffy: *The Stripping of the Altars*, p.123.
14   Quoted in Arnold, John, *Belief and Unbelief in Medieval Europe* (London, 2005), p.141.
15   Thomas: *Religion and the Decline of Magic*, p.191.
16   Volz, Carl, *The Medieval Church. From the Dawn of the Middle Ages to the Eve of the Reformation* (Nashville, 1997), p.147.
17   Duffy: *The Stripping of the Altars*, p.165.
18   Duffy: *The Stripping of the Altars*, p.179.
19   Recorded in Shinners: *Medieval Popular Religion 1000–1500*, pp.172–3.

Chapter Six – Contemporary and Medieval Christian Life

1   Ustorf, Werner, '"Not through the sound of thunder". The quest for God in the backyard of history', in F. Young (ed), *Dare We Speak of God in Public?* (London, 1995), pp.100–14. The section that follows is indebted to Ustorf's work.
2   Ustorf: '"Not through the sound of thunder". The quest for God in the backyard of history', pp.102–3.
3   'The faith of a Spanish peasant', in J. Shinners (ed), *Medieval Popular Religion 1000–1500. A Reader* (Ontario, 1997), pp.61, 62.
4   Duffy: *The Stripping of the Altars*, p.16.
5   What is being described here is similar to what Alan Billings means by the idea of 'cultural Christianity'. See his book: Billings, Alan, *Secular Lives, Sacred Hearts. The Role of the Church in a time of no religion* (London, 2004).

6   Davie, Grace, *Religion in Europe. A Memory Mutates* (Oxford, 2000), p.59.
7   Finucane, Ronald, *Miracles and Pilgrims. Popular Beliefs in Medieval England* (New York, 1977), p.46.
8   Duffy: *The Stripping of the Altars*, p.339.
9   Quoted in Shinners: *Medieval Popular Religion*, p.363.
10   Duffy: *The Stripping of the Altars*, p.357.

Chapter Seven – The Enlightenment Effect

1   Gay, Peter, *The Enlightenment: An Interpretation. Vol. I. The Rise of Modern Paganism* (New York, 1966); Gay: *The Enlightenment: An Interpretation. Vol. II. The Science of Freedom* (New York, 1969).
2   Gay: *The Enlightenment: An Interpretation. Vol. I*, p.17.
3   The term 'philosophes' is used as a collective noun to describe the diverse group of people who contributed to the Enlightenment. Gay describes them on his first page as 'a loose, informal, wholly unorganized coalition of cultural critics, religious sceptics, and political reformers from Edinburgh to Naples, Paris to Berlin, Boston to Philadelphia'. They included university philosophers, journalists, economists, cultural critics and politicians. No English word describes this group with the same accuracy and resonance.
4   The essay is printed in Hyland, Paul, with Gomez, Olga & Greensides, Francesca (eds), *The Enlightenment. A Sourcebook and Reader* (London, 2003), pp.54–8.
5   Hyland, with Gomez & Greensides: *The Enlightenment. A Sourcebook and Reader*, p.54.
6   Gay: *The Enlightenment: An Interpretation. Vol. I*, p.141.
7   Gay: *The Enlightenment: An Interpretation. Vol. I*, p.8.
8   Gay: *The Enlightenment: An Interpretation. Vol. I*, p.3.
9   Gay: *The Enlightenment: An Interpretation. Vol. I*, p.4.
10   These criticisms are surveyed by Dorinda Outram. Outram, Dorinda, *The Enlightenment*, 2nd edn (Cambridge, 2005).
11   See Gay: *The Enlightenment: An Interpretation. Vol. II*, especially Book Three, Chapter One, pp.3–55.
12   Cited in Gay: *The Enlightenment: An Interpretation. Vol. II*, p.9.
13   Gay: *The Enlightenment: An Interpretation. Vol. II*, pp.9–10.
14   Brief biographical details are available in Hyland, with Gomez & Greensides: *The Enlightenment. A Sourcebook and Reader*, pp.37–8.
15   Cited in Gay: *The Enlightenment: An Interpretation. Vol. II*, p.129.
16   Porter, Roy, *The Enlightenment*, 2nd edn (Basingstoke, 2001), p.15.

17   For this section, see Gay: *The Enlightenment: An Interpretation. Vol. II*, p.141f; and Hyland, with Gomez & Greensides: *The Enlightenment. A Sourcebook and Reader*, pp.37–8.

18   Hampson, Norman, *The Enlightenment. An evaluation of its assumptions, attitudes and values* (London, 1968), p.86.

19   Gay: *The Enlightenment: An Interpretation. Vol. II*, p.26.

20   Porter: *The Enlightenment*, pp.29–37.

21   Gay: *The Enlightenment: An Interpretation. Vol. I*, pp.201–2.

22   Siedentop, Larry, *Democracy in Europe* (London, 2001), especially Chapter Ten, pp.189–214; Gray, John, *Straw Dogs. Thoughts on Humans and Other Animals* (London, 2002); and Gray, John, *Enlightenment's Wake. Politics and Culture at the Close of the Modern Age* (London, 1995).

23   Siedentop: *Democracy in Europe*, p.197.

24   Siedentop: *Democracy in Europe*, p.210.

25   This is the approach adopted in Gray: *Straw Dogs*.

26   Gray: *Straw Dogs*, p.4.

27   Gray: *Straw Dogs*, p.31.

28   Gray: *Straw Dogs*, p.109.

Chapter Eight – The Last Puritan Age

1   Brown, Callum, *The Death of Christian Britain* (London, 2001), p.9.

2   Bruce is amongst those who argue the figure is at the lower end of the scale. Bruce, Steve, *Religion in the Modern World. From Cathedrals to Cults* (Oxford, 1996), p.30. Brown is more generous: Brown: *The Death of Christian Britain*, p.162.

3   Brown: *The Death of Christian Britain*, pp.156–61.

4   Brown: *The Death of Christian Britain*, pp.11–15.

5   Brown: *The Death of Christian Britain*, p.25.

6   Brown employs a methodology which is dependent on cultural theory. He calls the Christian identity he is investigating 'discursive Christianity'.

7   Brown: *The Death of Christian Britain*, pp.39–40.

8   Brown: *The Death of Christian Britain*, p.46.

9   Brown: *The Death of Christian Britain*, pp.49–50.

10   Royle, Edward, *Victorian Infidels. The Origins of the British Secularist Movement 1791–1866*, p.284.

11   Royle: *Victorian Infidels*, p.4.

12   Royle: *Victorian Infidels*, p.237.

13   Royle: *Victorian Infidels*, p.287.

14   This translation, cited in Kaufmann, Walter, *Nietzsche. Philosopher, Psychologist, Antichrist*, 4th edn (Princeton, 1974), p.97. The following discussion of the parable follows Kaufmann, pp.96–102.
15   Kaufmann, Walter, *Nietzsche*, p.101.

Chapter Nine – The Ethics Society

1   Martin, David, *On Secularization. Towards a Revised General Theory* (Aldershot, 2005).
2   Martin: *On Secularization*, pp.3–4.
3   Martin: *On Secularization*, p.119.
4   Martin makes the same point. See Martin: *On Secularization*, p.75.
5   Gray, John, *Straw Dogs. Thoughts on Humans and Other Animals* (London, 2002).
6   Gray: *Straw Dogs*, p.26.
7   Gray: *Straw Dogs*, p.28.
8   Gray: *Straw Dogs*, p.89.
9   Gray: *Straw Dogs*, p.92.
10   Gray: *Straw Dogs*, p.44.
11   Hauerwas has written a good number of books. I shall focus on one of these, which addresses directly the question of the liberal democratic order in the USA: Hauerwas, Stanley, *A Community of Character. Toward a Constructive Christian Social Ethic* (Notre Dame, 1981).
12   Hauerwas: *A Community of Character*, p.78.
13   Hauerwas: *A Community of Character*, p.83.
14   Hauerwas: *A Community of Character*, p.85.
15   The most insightful criticisms of both Hauerwas' ideas and his place in US culture come from Professor Jeffrey Stout. Stout has known Hauerwas a long time and is a detailed critic of his ideas and their inspiration. See especially Stout, Jeffrey, *Democracy and Tradition* (Princeton, 2004).
16   Stout: *Democracy and Tradition*, pp.2–3.
17   Stout: *Democracy and Tradition*, p.99.
18   Stout: *Democracy and Tradition*, p.3.

Bibliography

Arnold, John, *Belief and Unbelief in Medieval Europe* (London, 2005).
Arts, Wil, and Halman, Loek, *European Values at the Turn of the Millennium* (Leiden, 2004).
Barnwell, P.S., Cross, Claire, and Rycraft, Ann (eds), *Mass and Parish Life in Late Medieval England: The use of York* (Reading, 2005).
Berger, Peter, *The Sacred Canopy. Elements of a Sociological Theory of Religion* (New York, 1969).
Berger, Peter, *The Social Reality of Religion* (Harmondsworth, 1972).
Billings, Alan, *Secular Lives, Sacred Hearts* (London, 2004).
Blackmann, H.J., *Humanism* (Harmondsworth, 1968).
Bossy, John, *Christianity in the West 1400–1700* (Oxford, 1985).
Brierley, Peter, *The Tide is Running Out. What the English Church Attendance Survey Reveals* (London, 2000).
Briggs, Asa, *The Age of Improvement, 1783–1867* (London, 1959).
Brooke, Rosalind, and Brooke, Christopher, *Popular Religion in the Middle Ages. Western Europe 1000–1300* (London, 1984).
Brown, Callum, *The Death of Christian Britain* (London, 2001).
Brown, Peter, *Augustine of Hippo. A Biography* (Berkeley, [1967] 2000).
Brown, Peter, *The Cult of the Saints. Its Rise and Function in Latin Christianity* (London, 1981).
Bruce, Steve (ed), *Religion and Modernization. Sociologists and Historians debate the Secularization Thesis* (Oxford, 1992).
Bruce, Steve, *Religion in the Modern World. From Cathedrals to Cults* (Oxford, 1996).

Bruce, Steve, *God is Dead. Secularization in the West* (Oxford, 2002).

Burleigh, Michael, *Earthly Powers. Religion and Politics in Europe from the Enlightenment to the Great War* (London, 2005).

Burton, Janet, *Medieval Monasticism. Monasticism in the medieval West: from its origins to the coming of the friars* (Oxford, 1996).

Chadwick, Owen, *The Victorian Church*, 2 volumes (London, 1966–70).

Chadwick, Owen, *The Secularization of the European Mind in the 19th Century* (Cambridge, 1975).

Cox, Harvey, *The Secular City. Secularization and Urbanization in Theological Perspective* (London, 1965).

Davie, Grace, *Religion in Britain since 1945* (Oxford, 1994).

Davie, Grace, *Religion in Modern Europe. A Memory Mutates* (Oxford, 2000).

Davie, Grace, *Europe: The Exceptional Case. Parameters of Faith in the Modern World* (London, 2002).

Davie, Grace, Heelas, Paul, and Woodhead, Linda (eds), *Predicting Religion. Christian, Secular and Alternative Futures* (Ashgate, 2003).

Duffy, Eamon, *The Stripping of the Altars. Traditional Religion in England 1400–1580* (New Haven, 1992).

Dunn, John, *The Political Thought of John Locke: An Historical Account of the Argument of the 'Two Treatises of Government'* (Cambridge, 1969).

Dupré, Louis, *The Enlightenment and the Intellectual Foundations of Modern Culture* (New Haven, 2004).

Elliott-Binns, *Religion in the Victorian Era* (Cambridge, 1936).

Esposito, John, and Tamimi, Azzam (eds), *Islam and Secularism in the Middle East* (London, 2000).

Feuerbach, Ludwig, *The Essence of Christianity*, trans: Eliot, George (New York, [1841] 1989).

Finke, Roger, and Stark, Rodney, *The Churching of America, 1776–2005. Winners and Losers in Our Religious Economy* (New Brunswick, 2005).

Finucane, Ronald, *Miracles and Pilgrims. Popular Beliefs in Medieval England* (New York, 1977).

Forrester, Duncan, *Christian Justice and Public Policy* (Cambridge, 1997).

Fraser, Antonia, *Cromwell. Our Chief of Men* (London, 1973).

French, Katherine, *The People of the Parish: Community Life in a Late Medieval English Diocese* (Philadelphia, 2001).

Freud, Sigmund, *Totem and Taboo* in The Standard Edition of the Complete Psychological Works of Sigmund Freud, Vol. XIII (1913–1914), trans: Strachey, James (London, [1913] 1955).

Freud, Sigmund, *The Future of an Illusion* in The Standard Edition of the Complete Psychological Works of Sigmund Freud, Vol. XXI (1927–1931), trans: Strachey, James (London, [1927] 1964).

Fukuyama, Francis, *The End of History and the Last Man* (London, 1992).

Gay, Peter, *The Enlightenment: An Interpretation. Vol. I. The Rise of Modern Paganism* (New York, 1966).

Gay, Peter, *The Enlightenment: An Interpretation. Vol. II. The Science of Freedom* (New York, 1969).

Gay, Peter, *Freud. A Life for our Time* (New York, 1988).

Gibbon, Edward, *The Decline and Fall of the Roman Empire*, edited and abridged by Hugh Trevor-Roper (London, [1776] 1970).

Gilbert, Alan, *Religion and Society in Industrial England: Church, Chapel and Social Change, 1740–1914* (London, 1976).

Gilbert, Alan, *The Making of Post-Christian Britain* (London, 1980).

Gill, Robin, *The Empty Church Revisited* (Aldershot, 2003).

Gray, John, *Enlightenment's Wake. Politics and Culture at the Close of the Modern Age* (London, 1995).

Gray, John, *Straw Dogs. Thoughts on Humans and Other Animals* (London, 2002).

Halman, Loek, *The European Values Study: A Third Wave. Source book of the 1999/2000 European Values Study surveys* (Le Tilburg, 2001).

Hamilton, Bernard, *Religion in the Medieval West*, 2nd edn (London, 2002).

Hampson, Norman, *The Enlightenment. An Evaluation of its Assumptions, Attitudes and Values* (London, 1968).

Hastings, Adrian, *A History of English Christianity, 1920–1985* (London, 1986).

Hauerwas, Stanley, *A Community of Character. Toward a Constructive Christian Social Ethic* (Notre Dame, 1981).

Hauerwas, Stanley, *With the Grain of the Universe. The Church's Witness and Natural Theology* (London, 2002).

Hillgarth, J.N. (ed), *Christianity and Paganism, 350–750. The Conversion of Western Europe*, revised edn (Philadelphia, 1986).

Hobsbwan, Eric, *The Age of Capital, 1848–1875* (London, 1975).

Hoffman Berman, Constance, *Medieval Religion. New Approaches* (London, 2005).

Hyland, Paul, with Gomez, Olga, and Greensides, Francesca (eds), *The Enlightenment. A Sourcebook and Reader* (London, 2003).

Jacoby, Susan, *Freethinkers. A History of American Secularism* (New York, 2004).

Jones, Rufus, 'Secular Civilization and the Christian Task' in *The Christian Life and Message in relation to Non-Christian Systems. Report of the Jerusalem Meeting of the International Missionary Council, 24 March to 8 April 1928, Vol. 1* (London, 1928), pp.284–338.

Kaufmann, Walter, *Nietzsche. Philosopher, Psychologist, Antichrist*, 4th edn (Princeton, 1974).

Kenny, Anthony, *A Brief History of Western Philosophy* (Oxford, 1998).

Lawrence, C.H., *Medieval Monasticism. Forms of Religious Life in Western Europe in the Middle Ages*, 3rd edn (Harlow, 2001).

Lindbeck, George, *The Nature of Doctrine. Religion and Theology in a Postliberal Age* (Philadelphia, 1984).

Locke, John, *Two Treatises of Government*, ed Goldie, Mark (London, [1689] 1993).

Macquarrie, John, *God and Secularity. New Directions in Theology Today*, Vol. III (London, 1968).

Martin, David, *A General Theory of Secularization* (Oxford, 1978).

Martin, David, *On Secularization. Towards a Revised General Theory* (Aldershot, 2005).

McLeod, Hugh, *Secularisation in Western Europe, 1848–1914* (New York, 2002).

McLeod, Hugh, and Ustorf, Werner, *The Decline of Christendom in Western Europe, 1750–2000* (Cambridge, 2003).

Milbank, John, *Theology and Social Theory. Beyond Secular Reason* (Oxford, 1990).

Mitchell, Joshua, *Not By Reason Alone. Religion, History, and Identity in Early Modern Political Thought* (Chicago, 1993).

Morris, Jeremy, 'The Strange Death of Christian Britain: Another Look at the Secularization Debate', *The Historical Journal*, 46/4 (Cambridge, 2003), pp.963–76.

Nehamas, Alexander, *Nietzsche. Life as Literature* (London, 1985).

Newbigin, Lesslie, *The Gospel in a Pluralist Society* (London, 1989).

Niebuhr, H. Richard, *Christ and Culture* (New York, 1951).

Nineham, Dennis, *Christianity Mediaeval and Modern. A Study in Religious Change* (London, 1993).

Norman, Edward, *Church and Society in England, 1770–1970, A Historical Study* (Oxford, 1976).

Norman, Edward, *Secularisation. Sacred Values in a Godless World* (London, 2002).

Obelkevich, James (ed), *Religion and the People 800–1700* (Chapel Hill, 1979).

Outram, Dorinda, *The Enlightenment*, 2nd edn (Cambridge, 2005).

Percy, Martyn, *The Salt of the Earth. Religious Resilience in a Secular Age* (London, 2001).

Plant, Raymond, *Politics, Theology and History* (Cambridge, 2001).

Porter, Roy, *The Enlightenment*, 2nd edn (Basingstoke, 2001).

Raiser, Konrad, *Ecumenism in Transition. A Paradigm Shift in the Ecumenical Movement* (Geneva, 1991).

Rawls, John, *Political Liberalism* (New York, 1996).

Rawls, John, *A Theory of Justice*, revised edn (Oxford, 1999).

Royle, Edward, *Victorian Infidels. The Origins of the British Secularist Movement 1791–1866* (Manchester, 1974).

Scruton, Roger, *Kant. A Very Short Introduction*, revised edn (Oxford, 2001).

Shinners, John (ed), *Medieval Popular Relgion 1000–1500. A Reader* (Ontario, 1997).

Siedentop, Larry, *Democracy in Europe* (London, 2000).

Southern, R.W., *Western Society and the Church in the Middle Ages* (London, 1970).

Stouck, Mary-Ann (ed), *Medieval Saints. A Reader* (Ontario, 1999).

Stout, Jeffrey, *Democracy and Tradition* (Princeton, 2004).

Sykes, Richard, *Popular Religion in Dudley and the Gornals, c. 1914–1965* (unpublished University of Wolverhampton PhD thesis, 1999).

Sykes, Stephen, *The Identity of Christianity. Theologians and the Essence of Christianity from Schleiermacher to Barth* (London, 1984).

Thacker, Alan, and Sharpe, Richard (ed), *Local Saints and Local Churches in the Early Medieval West* (Oxford, 2002).

Thomas, Keith, *Religion and the Decline of Magic. Studies in Popular Beliefs in Sixteenth and Seventeeth-Century England* (London, 1973).

Thrower, James, *Western Atheism. A Short History* (New York, [1971] 2000).

Ustorf, Werner, 'Not through the sound of thunder', The quest for God in the backyard of history, in Young, Frances (ed), *Dare We Speak of God in Public?* (London, 1995), pp.100–14.

Voltaire, *Candide* (London, [1759] 1997).

Volz, Carl, *The Medieval Church. From the Dawn of the Middle Ages to the Eve of the Reformation* (Nashville, 1997).

Weber, Max, *The Protestant Ethic and the Spirit of Capitalism*, trans. Parsons, Talcott (London, [1930] 1992).

Williams, Sarah, *Religious Belief and Popular Culture*, in Williams, Sarah, *Religious Belief and Popular Culture in Southwark, c. 1880–1939* (Oxford, 1999).

Wilson, Bryan, *Religion in Secular Society* (London, 1966).

Young, Frances (ed), *Dare We Speak of God in Public?* (London, 1995).

Index